# From Headrack To Claude

## Collected Gay Comix
### by HOWARD CRUSE

Nifty Kitsch PRESS
NORTH ADAMS, MA

## Communiqué

ONE NIGHT RECENTLY I WOKE UP MUTTERING **UNEARTHLY SYLLABLES**...

PLOZNOON SNRASH TREL KLARBBORY LAKKIL GY CHEFFR!

BROPPLE ZIX ZNOGBROL!

WHY ARE YOU **TYPING** AT THREE IN THE MORNING, HOWIE?

YOU WON'T **BELIEVE** THIS, EDDIE, BUT I'M RECEIVING SOME KIND OF **TELEPATHIC COMMUNIQUE** IN A LANGUAGE NEVER HEARD BY **HUMAN EARS!** IT'S VERY CRUCIAL THAT I WRITE IT ALL DOWN!

CLACK! CLACK! CLACK!

WHAT SLOWLY DAWNED ON ME DURING THE WEEKS OF TRANSCRIPTION THAT FOLLOWED WAS THAT A **LEARNED BEING** FROM **ANOTHER DIMENSION** WAS SENDING ME **URGENT INSTRUCTIONS** ON HOW TO DIVERT THE HUMAN RACE FROM ITS CURRENT PATH TOWARD **NUCLEAR CATASTROPHE**...

FRENK HWUNT!

PREK ZKYZ!

GHREE BOLORL FLOB! (TSK! TSK!)

POOPUNE WHREBL SIPPBIBB!

A THOUSAND PAGES OF MANUSCRIPT LATER...

THIS IS PROBABLY THE MOST **IMPORTANT BOOK** OF OUR **CENTURY!** I'M GOING TO MAIL IT TO A **MAJOR BOOK PUBLISHER** RIGHT AWAY!

COULD YOU PICK UP SOME **MILK** ON THE WAY BACK FROM THE POST OFFICE?

IT FILLS ME WITH **HUMILITY** TO THINK THAT **I** WAS SELECTED TO TRANSMIT THIS **AWESOME MESSAGE** TO HUMANITY!

MAYBE PEOPLE WILL TAKE ME **SERIOUSLY** NOW INSTEAD OF WRITING ME OFF AS JUST SOME DINKY **COMIC BOOK ARTIST!**

I WONDER IF I'LL GET TO GO ON **TV TALK SHOWS**...

TAKE A LOOK AT THIS **GARBAGE**, PETE! "...PLOK MLUM ZY GLOYK; VWENZ TRELLOR (ARL HEZFZUN OL!) PRYKKN, HAF PIUL, LOLBR—FFYIK PAYP: TU NUBBNO LRAK, POBB!..."

GOD, YOU'RE **RIGHT**, LILY—THAT'S THE WORST JOB OF PUNCTUATION I'VE SEEN ALL **YEAR!**

EDITORIAL DEPT.

WHY EDITORS GET GRAY.

There's no substantive gay content in the surreal strip above. Still, I enjoyed tossing a few throwaway images of Eddie's and my home life into the mix as a way of injecting some mild queer visibility into the heterosexuality-saturated pages of *Heavy Metal*.

**Other books
by Howard Cruse**

*Stuck Rubber Baby*
*Felix's Friends*
*The Complete Wendel*

and with Jeanne E. Shaffer...
*The Swimmer With a Rope in His Teeth*

**Nifty Kitsch PRESS**

FROM HEADRACK TO CLAUDE is published in July 2009 by Lulu.com under the author's own Nifty Kitsch Press imprint. Inquiries about this work may be directed to the author by email (howard@howardcruse.com) or by regular mail sent to P.O. Box 100, North Adams, MA 01247, USA.

ISBN: 978-0-578-03251-1

# Contents

*Not gay, but what the hell!

**AUTHOR'S NOTE:** Since some satirical references in this book take jabs or poke fun at people or past events that by now may no longer ring a bell, you'll occasionally find me hovering over your shoulder whispering explanations in your ear. If you find this annoying, feel free to ignore me.

# Acknowledgments

**Thank you** to Denis Kitchen for suggesting and publishing *Gay Comix* and for inviting me to serve as its founding editor.

**Thank you** to Robert Triptow and Andy Mangels, who successively assumed the editorship of *Gay Comix* (renamed *Gay Comics* during Andy's stewardship) after I left the series to concentrate on my comic strip *Wendel*.

**Thank you** to Charles Ortleb and Tom Steele, respectively the publisher and editor of *Christopher Street*, who broadened the reach of my *Gay Comix* stories by reprinting them in that groundbreaking literary magazine.

**Thank you** to Richard Goldstein, former Executive Editor at *The Village Voice*, and George Delmerico, the *Voice*'s former Design Director, for welcoming me into the weekly's pages in 1981 and providing me maximum creative freedom in the topical comic strips that I contributed; and to subsequent art directors Ted Keller and Minh Uong for giving me additional assignments for the *Voice* after George's departure.

**Thank you** to David Frankel, former editor of *Artforum International*, who provided space for "Homoeroticism Blues" in that prestigious magazine.

**Thank you** to Trina Robbins, Robert Triptow, and Bill Sienkiewicz, co-editors of *Strip AIDS USA*, for including "The Woeful World of Winnie and Walt" in that fundraising anthology benefitting San Francisco's Shanti Project; and to Debbie Delano and Phyllis Moore, co-editors and publishers of *AARGH* (Artists Against Rampant Goverrnment Homophobia), which raised funds to fight for repeal of Clause 28 in Great Britain.

**Thank you** to the late Paul Taylor, who prompted the creation of "1986: An Interim Epilogue," which was published as an addendum to the reprinting of "Safe Sex" in Australia's *Art & Text* magazine.

**Thank you** to Tim Fish, the editor of *Young Bottoms in Love*, and to Robert Kirby and David Kelly, co-editors of *Born to Trouble: The Book of Boy Trouble 2*, for including "My Hypnotist" and "Then There Was Claude" respectively in those two anthologies; and to Ed Mathews of the web site Popimage.com, without whose subsidy "My Hypnotist" could not have been drawn and who provided an online showcase to the entire *Young Bottoms in Love* series prior to its publication in book form.

**Thank you** to Dr. Ralph Blair, founding editor of the *Homosexual Counseling Journal*, who encouraged me to take a deep breath and risk addressing gay concerns in a published cartoon for the first time back in 1974.

**Thank you** to Dale Hopson for letting me use his photograph of George Segal's "Gay Liberation" statues at Sheridan Square.

And finally...

**A big thank you** to my husband, Ed Sedarbaum, for his unwavering support and encouragement during all these years since we joined forces in 1979, as well as apologies for using a fictionalized version of him as a foil in my cartoons from time to time.

Howard Cruse
July 2009

# Preface

This book is called *From Headrack to Claude* in recognition of the two characters bearing those names whose stories serve as bookends for the 33 years covered by this comix compilation.

Headrack, an artist of vaulting ambition and unlimited insecurity, was an ongoing character in my *Barefootz* series from its 1971 inception onward. Roughly midway through the eight-year period during which *Barefootz* was my dominant vehicle for expression in the comix form, Headrack came out of the closet in an explosion of long-repressed liberationist fury that appeared in the second issue of *Barefootz Funnies*.

"Claude," my fictionalized version of a sexy ministerial student with whom I had a brief romance early in my own period of youthful self-discovery, appears as my bedpartner in a 2008 memory strip called "Then There Was Claude," which was included in last year's *Book of Boy Trouble Volume 2*. The character's presence in the overall Howard Cruse *oeuvre* is noticeably fleeting compared to Headrack's, but as the co-star of my most recently drawn gay-themed comic to date, Claude gets the honor by default of being the companion bookend to Headrack in my book's title.

Headrack's "coming out" vehicle, a twelve-page story entitled "Gravy on Gay," was a major turning point for the *Barefootz* series and a harbinger of a second big turning point for me that came three years later when I announced that I planned to serve as editor for *Gay Comix* and that I was gay myself. Yet despite the important role that Headrack's outing played in shaping my artistic development thereafter, the story has never been re-printed until now. The reasons for this omission are largely technical, having to do with the arrival of the digital age, the uneasy relationship between scanners and heavily-Zipatoned* comic-book art, and the understandable abandonment by Fantagraphics Books on commercial grounds of what would have been a companion volume to 1990's *Early Barefootz* had that book enjoyed better sales numbers.

With this book I'm attempting to assemble in a single package all of the gay-themed comics I've ever published. Now would seem to be the time, therefore, to give "Gravy on Gay" its proper place at the front of the line. The Zipatone problem has now been overcome by laborious use of Adobe Photoshop tools augmented by adhesive-unhinging heat applied by a hair-dryer (don't ask), so that the tones in the story look even better here than they did the first time around.

Many readers of this book will have first encountered my comics in 1980, when *Gay Comix* arrived in LGBT bookstores, if not later on when my *Wendel* series became a regular feature in *The Advocate*, when my graphic novel *Stuck Rubber Baby* appeared in 1995, or when I began to achieve visibility in other venues outside of 1970s underground comic books. For these readers, the very drawing style of my Headrack story may be disorienting. Why in the world would the guy behind *Wendel* and *Stuck Rubber Baby* have peopled his first gay story with characters so cartoony and oddly proportioned?

It took many pages to fully describe what lay behind the *Barefootz* style when I attempted to do so in my preface to *Early Barefootz*, so I won't even try to accomplish that degree of illumination in a paragraph here. But in the pages that follow I am providing at least some background information in the form of illustrated, scrapbook-like summaries called *Artifacts & Benchmarks, Parts 1 and 2* that will hopefully put my creative decisions in context. The first of these interpolations describes the years of experimentation, groping, and political awakening that led up to "Gravy on Gay"; the second recounts the interval between Headrack's public coming out and my own, including the career pressures that raised the stakes in taking that step.

Aside from the *Barefootz*-related exposition alluded to above, the comics in this book fall into three categories: my stories drawn for *Gay Comix*; my short topical strips addressing passing controversies; and my most recent stories drawn after the years spent focusing on *Wendel* and *Stuck Rubber Baby*. There is some chronological over-lap in these categories, but I am separating them into different sections because of their very different purposes, styles, and places in my career.

Howard Cruse
July 2009

---

*"Zipatone," a trademarked term—commonly used as a generic, to the trademark-holder's frustration, I'm sure—that refers to sheets of transparent, adhesive-backed film with half-tone dots of varying sizes printed on them. This tool was frequently applied to selected portions of original cartoon artwork in the pre-digital age to achieve the illusion of gray areas that in reality contained only purely white and purely black components.

## FROM MISS THING TO JANE'S WORLD

Miss Thing
art by Joe
Johnson

**A**s most readers of this book will almost certainly know, I'm far from the only LGBT cartoonist who has put in time drawing comic strips and stories about the gay experience. Indeed, a fresh crew of exciting queer comics artists began putting their points of view onto paper immediately on the heels of *Gay Comix*'s debut, and some (like Mary Wings, Roberta Gregory, Lee Marrs, and the contributors to *Gay Heartthrobs*, the first gay male comix anthology) had already started the ball rolling before I arrived on the scene. In fact, the work of Wings, Gregory, and Marrs helped solidify my own sense of what kind of comic I hoped *Gay Comix* could be.

**A**nd then there was Joe Johnson, whose *Miss Thing* was flouncing through pages of *The Advocate* well before the patrons of the Stonewall Inn got around to rioting.

**B**y now there are too many LGBT artists regularly expressing themselves in the comics form for anyone to keep up with. Their work can be found in anthologies like *Boy Trouble* and *Juicy Mother*, in indy 'zines and mini-comix, in local LGBT and alternative newspapers, on the Web, in high-end books that I haven't even heard about yet, and in modest self-publishing ventures that have received funding from the Xeric Foundation or other sources of subsidy or by the kind of raids on personal savings that dedicated artists throughout history have often been forced to resort to.

**I**t's demonstrated ever more frequently that queer comic creators no longer need to make peace with cultural marginalization, what with Alison Bechdel's graphic memoir *Fun Home* having gained best-sellerdom among mainstream audiences and been named 2006's Best Book of the Year by Time.com.

**M**any LGBT cartoonists deserve to be cited by name, but a lot of them are my friends and I don't dare talk about some for fear I'll accidentally leave others out. Fortunately, anyone who'd like a fuller overview of today's LGBT comics works and creators can turn to great online resources like Prism Comics and The Gay Comics List.* There are no doubt others, but these will get you started.

*Jane's World* art
©2003 by Paige Braddock
www.janecomics.com

*www.prismcomics.org and http://gaycomicslist.free.fr/pages/welcome.php, respectively

As we ambled idly onto **CHRISTOPHER STREET**, we happened upon a **DISTURBANCE**...

**R**iots or no riots, becoming an openly gay cartoonist wasn't on my mind that June night in Greenwich Village.

## That Night at the Stonewall

**by Howard Cruse**

**TRUE STORY:** It was **1969**. Some friends and I had dropped **ACID** that night and sprawled on the grass of Central Park for a **TINY TIM CONCERT**...

*We'll trip the light fantasy*

*the sidewalks of New York*

Afterwards we taxied back downtown to continue our trip in the **VILLAGE**...

...WHAT I'M SAYING IS — **AUTOMOTIVE TRANSPORT** IS JUST A **SLOW** FORM OF **INTER-SPACIAL 'BEAMING'!**

EASY THERE, CAPTAIN KIRK!

SAY, LOOK AT ALL THE **ANDROIDS** ON THE STREET!

FALAFEL! I'M **STARVING** FOR FALAFEL!!

FUCKIN' HIPPIES...

©1982 H. Cruse

As we ambled idly onto **CHRISTOPHER STREET**, we happened upon a **DISTURBANCE**...

DO I SEE SOMETHING **DRAMATIC** AFOOT?

C'MON, HOWIE... LET'S GO **WATCH!**

WHAT GIVES?

There was a **FUROR** erupting in front of the **STONEWALL INN**, one of my gay haunts of choice.

We strolled up to the periphery of the action amid the **YELLS, POLICE SIRENS** and **FLYING BOTTLES**, watching it all as though it were a **PSYCHEDELIC STAGE PLAY** that posed no danger to us at all...

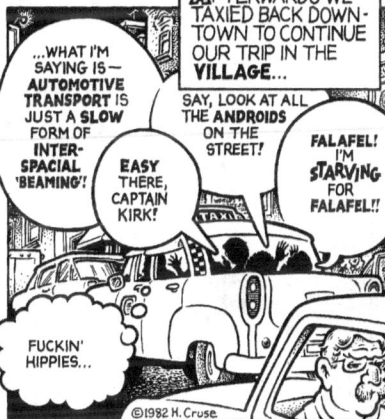

??

FAR OUT!

*INTERESTING!

ASSHOLES!

CRASH!

PIGS!

In our hallucinatory states of mind, it was hard to be sure how **REAL** the riot was, or what was its **SIGNIFICANCE**. Were we witnessing the **REVOLUTION** that radicals had been predicting? Were **GOVERNMENTS** about to **FALL**? Was the **SOCIAL ORDER** being **UPENDED**?

We finally wandered away from the melee, not certain exactly **WHAT** we'd seen, or whether a **WHOLE NEW WORLD** had been ushered in before our eyes!

IT HAD!

GAY PRIDE

LISTEN, THIS GUY WAS **THERE!!**

WELL, IN A MANNER OF SPEAKING...

First published in *The Village Voice*

7

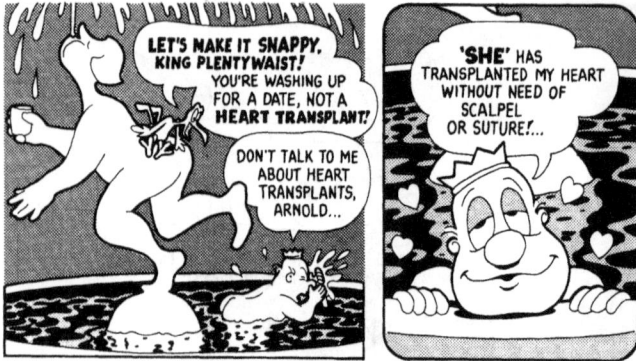

Above: Panels from one of my many stabs at newspaper syndication.

**T**here in New York in the summer of 1969 I was preoccupied with deciding whether I had what it took to make it as a cartoonist at all.

And if I did, what kind of cartoonist was I going to be?

At right: My exciting advertising art for a Birmingham car dealership.

**W**as I going to continue setting my sights on the kind of conventional cartooning career I had dreamed of since my childhood—chasing mundane freelance illustration gigs until some newspaper syndicate saw fit to give me my own daily comic strip—or was I going to heed the call of my acid visions and cast my lot with the counterculture?

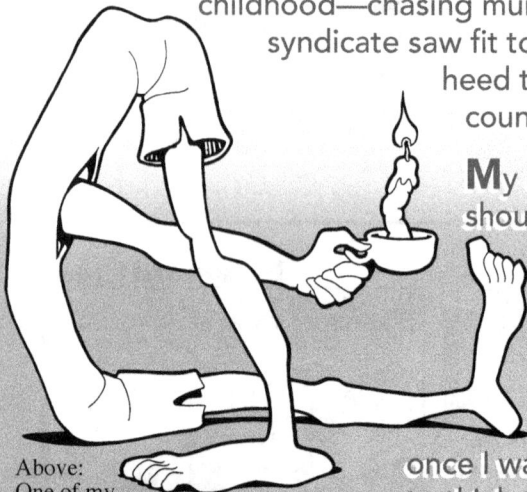

**M**y competing impulses over what my long-term goals should be continued to dog me after I moved back to Birmingham in the fall of 1969. And watching Gay Liberation gain ground in distant cities without my involvement added to my ongoing restlessness.

**F**alling in love with Don Higdon, an Alabama tripping buddy who quickly became a soul-mate, once I was back down south helped me get centered enough to think things through. The tranquility of our four years together freed my mind to discover my inner Barefootz! It also helped flush the last remnants of internalized homophobia out of my system.

Above: One of my early-1970s mash-ups between a traditional cartooning style and psychedelic improvisation.

Above: Me with Don, enjoying a John-and-Yoko *Two Virgins* moment.

At right: An early version of Barefootz, the acid-influenced doodle that became an exercise in intermingled innocence, allegory and trippiness and ultimately landed me in underground comic books.

**TOPS & BUTTON**

HEY, BUTTON, ARE YOU GONNA BE **INDOORS** OR **OUTDOORS** THIS AFTERNOON?

I'M NOT SURE...

I ALWAYS HAVE TROUBLE DECIDING BETWEEN DOORS.

Above: Drawing a daily cartoon about squirrels for the *Birmingham Post-Herald* for two years showed me what drawing for syndication might be like.

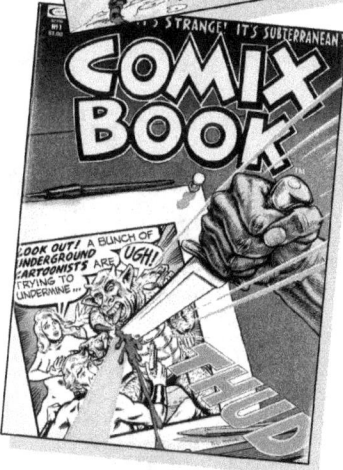

Sadly, Don and I went our separate ways in 1974, but the special, spiritually exploratory spirit that characterized our four years together had a lasting impact that's clearly traceable throughout the run of my *Barefootz* series, which was born in the pages of the University of Alabama *Crimson-White* and thereafter migrated among a succession of Birmingham-area underground newspapers until Denis Kitchen of Kitchen Sink Comix found some *Barefootz* samples that I sent him in 1972 amusing enough to begin including my feature in underground comix such as *Snarf*, *Bizarre Sex*, and other Kitchen Sink titles.

Then in 1974, when Stan Lee of Marvel Comics fame had a go at showcasing underground cartoonists in *Comix Book*, a quasi-mainstream magazine that Denis had signed on to edit, *Barefootz* was invited along for the ride.

By that time I no longer saw my Barefootz world merely as a vehicle for humorous weirdness. It was an extended allegory populated by a repertory troupe of players perfectly tailored for social and political satire, observations about interpersonal relationships, and explorations of the very nature of reality (this last being an especially common preoccupation among folks who had done a lot of acid-tripping). Introducing gay issues into the mix was also on my agenda.

Above: A panel from "The Boss Bug," a story spoofing the illusory underpinnings of the social order that I drew for the first issue of *Comix Book*.

Barefootz's mysterious "pet" Glory lived under the bed and harbored strange powers.

Barefootz was easy-going and likeable, but somehow not "of this earth."

The cockroaches who shared Barefootz's apartment represented humanity at its most chotic and unreflective.

Dolly was helplessly in the sway of her libido.

Headrack, a perpetually frustrated and underappreciated artist, was a supporting player in my *Barefootz* series. He had so much in common with me that I decided he *had* to be gay!

9

Above: One of my rehearsals for engaging a scary subject was my 1976 try at building a comic strip around a goofy gay couple.

As I planned for my venture into gay subject matter I was anything but fearless, as the subtext of my strip "The Passer-by" (which I drew in 1975 but never published) suggests. Its gist is unmistakable: How much of his interior life can someone shovel out for the world to see without sending others fleeing for cover?

**B**arefootz *Funnies* #1, my first solo comic book, saw print in 1975, by which time, despite my trepidations, I had definitely made up my mind that Headrack's coming-out story would be a backup feature in the second issue, which I planned to publish the following year.

10

The decision was made; now I just had to do it, and I had already gone so far as to court—in low-stakes settings or in oblique, non-committal ways—public speculation about my orientation.

To wit: In January of 1974 my first gay-themed cartoon of any sort (see below) was published in a low-risk corner of the world that no comix reader was likely to stumble on: the debut issue of *Homosexual Counseling Journal*, a publication aimed at individuals in the counseling professions, that was founded by Dr. Ralph Blair, a pioneer in psychological counseling for gay people with whom I had become friends while in grad school.

## FAMOUS GUILT SYNDROMES

THIS IS **TERRIBLE!** THEY'RE **ASSAULTING** OUR SENSIBILITIES!

SOMEBODY HAD BETTER REPORT **THIS** TO **GOD!**

**ACTUALLY**, I'D RATHER NOT GET **INVOLVED...**

CLENCH YOUR **EYEBALLS,** MORTIMER!

**Committing a Crime Against Nature**

Above: the intrepid underground cartoonist masquerades as a responsible paste-up artist for a prestigious Birmingham ad agency even as he prepares to risk all by announcing to the world that he is an unapologetic sodomite.

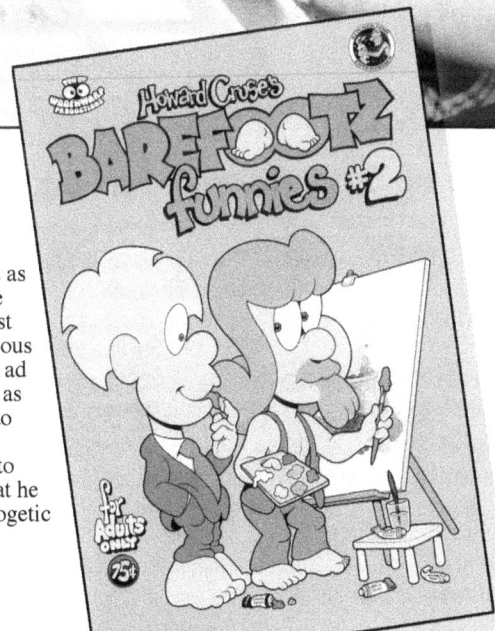

Then there was that mischievous footnote in my 1974 strip "Big Marvy's Tips on Tooth Care" (a treatise in *Snarf* #6 on the merits of brushing one's teeth with one's own ejaculate), which was guaranteed to arouse suspicion.

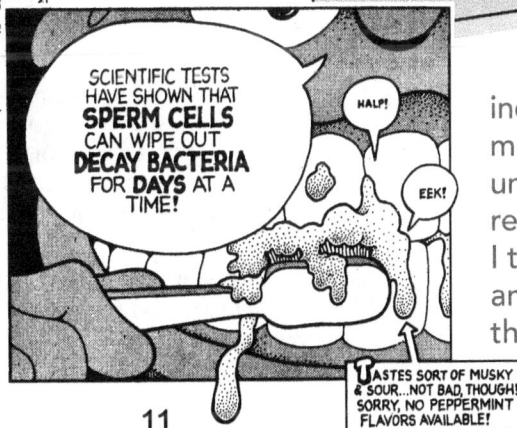

SCIENTIFIC TESTS HAVE SHOWN THAT **SPERM CELLS** CAN WIPE OUT **DECAY BACTERIA** FOR **DAYS** AT A TIME!

HALP!

EEK!

TASTES SORT OF MUSKY & SOUR...NOT BAD, THOUGH! SORRY, NO PEPPERMINT FLAVORS AVAILABLE!

The sky didn't fall in response to those indiscretions and my membership in the underground wasn't rescinded. So in 1976 I took a deep breath and plunged into the unknown with "Gravy on Gay."

11

**BACKSTORY**

### About **"Gravy on Gay"**

First of all, do not waste valuable brain cells trying to tease any significance out of the title "Gravy on Gay." There is none and never was. Just as sopranos, with or without hair, are nowhere to be found in Eugene Ionesco's absurdist comedy *The Bald Soprano*, no gravy is served to anyone in "Gravy on Gay," even at the diner where Mort behaves so unforgivably. I needed to call the story something, and "Gravy on Gay" popped out of some corner of my brain fully formed and, in its way, kind of interesting. So I ran with it.

There's no denying that "Gravy on Gay" is rude and crude to a degree that makes me cringe a bit now. When I first showed it to a cousin of mine, she remarked, "This is the angriest thing I've ever seen you draw!" While I intended it to be an uncharacteristically vehement and disturbing entry in the usually more low-key *Barefootz* canon, I hadn't realized how churning with internal fury I was over the many ways that casual societal homophobia, as embodied by the character Mort, had been violently jerking my emotions this way and that since I realized around the age of eleven that I was likely to become that most monstrous of beings: a homosexual.

But besides giving vent to real grievances, I was also responding to peer pressure. Being aggressively indecorous was prized behavior in the locker-room culture that dominated underground comix, and to some degree I was trying in the second issue of *Barefootz Funnies* to prove, to myself as much as to others, that I was not the prisoner of wussiness that the generally gentle style of humor in *Barefootz* had led some to accuse me of being.

I probably wouldn't come up with quite the same approach if I were to try and express the same feelings today. But I had a lot of shit to get out of my system in 1976 and, for better or for worse, this is the form that shit took when I splattered it onto the pages of my comic book.

### Who's that hovering outside the drugstore window?

The unexplained flying figure you see peeking into the splash panel of "Gravy on Gay" was derived from a nearly nude photo of my lover Don Higdon. It could be seen lurking somewhere in most of the *Barefootz* stories I drew in the 1970s (and in some subsequent non-*Barefootz* stories as well—like "I Always Cry at Movies," which you'll find elsewhere in this collection).

I used to refer to this floating icon as my "cosmic Alfred E. Newman." To quote from my preface to *Early Barefootz*, "The figure suggested something mysterious and joyous to me. He was a visitor from some other, more naturalistic plane of reality, briefly penetrating the *Barefootz* world. In a comic strip populated by beings who sported huge heads and tiny bodies, the figure was provocatively out of place. By his very presence he said, 'Don't be too sure you know what's going on. It may be something else entirely.'"

And now let's dip a toe into the GAY SUBCULTURE with Barefootz's good buddy

# Headrack

by Howard Cruse

in "GRAVY ON GAY"

13

Published in *Barefootz Funnies*

I'VE BEEN STANDING BY TOO LONG WITHOUT **COMMITTING** MY **ART** TO THE STRUGGLE!

AFTER ALL, IF THE **ARTIST** DOESN'T IGNITE THE BEACON OF SOCIAL ENLIGHTENMENT —WHO **WILL?**

GREAT ART ON SALE CHEAP (INSIDE)

I MUST CAPTURE THE **FERVID FLAME** OF **LIBERATION** IN ALL ITS **RAINBOWED SPLENDOR!**

WHAT'S **THIS?** *LAVENDER??*

**AWAY** WITH STEREOTYPIC HUES!

MY CANVAS MUST BURN WITH THE GLOW OF **TRUTH ALONE!**

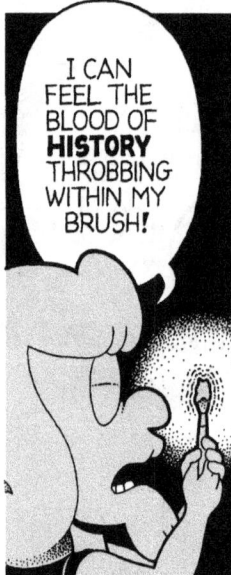

I CAN FEEL THE BLOOD OF **HISTORY** THROBBING WITHIN MY BRUSH!

I MEAN, WHEN I THINK OF ALL THE **SUFFERING** THAT'S GONE DOWN OVER THE YEARS...

SNIFF!

SAY, MAYBE THEY'LL WANT TO RUN A **REPRO** OF THIS IN **AFTER DARK!**...

ALL THE **SHIT**...

SOB!

14

15

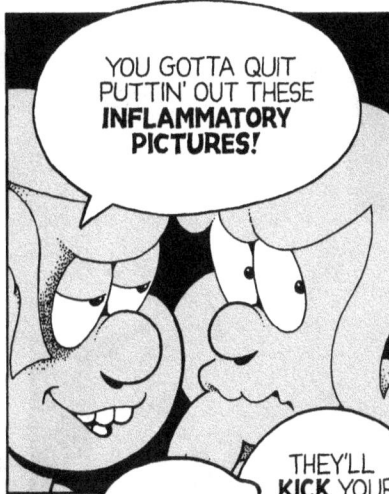

Even when you know that remaining closeted is a dead end, it's not easy to discard the strokes that go with being assumed to be heterosexual.

For example, any guts I may have exhibited by drawing "Gravy on Gay" were undercut by the final panel of my 1976 strip "How Barefootz Was Created," in which I back-slid by giving myself an unidentified female "beard" without quite admitting to myself that that's what I was doing.

Meanwhile, I was drawing flack from my underground cartooning peers over the "cute" look of my *Barefootz* gang, which was turning out to be more of a roadblock to my lofty vision for the series than I had anticipated.

And I had to admit that, as satisfying as it had been to vent my spleen in "Gravy on Gay," the character designs that I had originally chosen for my *Barefootz* universe didn't mesh well with my growing inclination to tackle gritty, real-world issues in my comic book stories.

Above: A self-accusatory sketchbook drawing that reflected my angst.

Above: Violence abruptly spawns chaos in this scene from a never-finished *Barefootz* story.

Some of the solutions that I contemplated were drastic, such as a plot turn I briefly toyed with in which the strip's entire cast would be assassinated, thus allowing me to replace them with more normally proportioned "actors."

**E**arly in 1977, shortly after *Barefootz Funnies* #2 saw print, I moved back to New York City for my second try at forging a "real" cartooning career.

**T**hings were shaky for me at first in the Big Apple, but an art directing job at *Starlog* kept me afloat until I had gained the contacts I needed to become a full-time freelancer.

**A**ll the while I continued the efforts I had begun back in Alabama to expand my comix-creating horizons beyond the increasingly apparent limitations of my *Barefootz* approach.

**I** also found doors unexpectedly opening to me at straight men's sex magazines.

DON'T PANIC, EVERYBODY! I'LL TAKE HIM INTO THE BACK ROOM AND 'TALK HIM DOWN'!

YOU'RE A LIFE-SAVER, CURTIS!

wink!

GORBLE JERKLE MRUMFUMP...

HI, MISS SPITUSI... REMEMBER ME??

WHY, IT'S LITTLE GOFER, ISN'T IT..?

...FROM THE SEVENTH ROW?

**N**ext I wished that I could fuck my fifth-grade teacher, who was always drivin' me crazy!

*"How cute! A fold-out!"*

**T**hat development made me uneasy, since I generally supported the Women's Movement and the dominant stance among feminists in those days was that porn images objectified women and were therefore unacceptable.

Still, when you're trying to get a career launched, finding publications who'll publish your work *at all* is a major struggle, and for me it was a natural leap from underground comix to sex-focused men's magazines, both of which rewarded sexual outrageousness. The best middle ground I could come up with was trying my best to keep my big-busted-naked-lady cartoons as playfully sex-positive and non-denigrating as possible within porn conventions.

Above: A panel from one of my parodies (©1979 by *Playboy*).

**T**hings got classier when *Playboy* invited me to create spoofs of mainstream comic strips for its new "Playboy Funnies" section. The pay was the best I had ever had, no naked ladies were required, and my friends were hugely impressed to see me in the famous magazine's pages. The constant changes demanded by Hugh Hefner, unfortunately, took a toll on my morale. I was happy to cash every *Playboy* check that arrived from Chicago, but I missed the creative freedom I had become accustomed to in underground comix.

**M**eanwhile, the dynamics of my personal life took a turn for the better when I fell in love with a lifelong New Yorker named Ed Sedarbaum, with whom I've shared my life ever since.

**B**esides reintroducing romance into my life, Eddie helped me grope my way through the thorny career dilemmas that were dogging me—like how to square my goal of being open to colleagues and fans about my gayness with the role hetero-centric humor was playing in my career.

**I**t's not that I begrudge straight guys their laffs. I'm pro-sex as a matter of principle and believe heterosexuals have as much right to enjoy their sexual fantasies as I do to enjoy mine. What made me feel compromised was knowing that simply by drawing for these markets I was encouraging readers to assume that I was straight like them. It didn't seem honest, somehow.

Photo credit: Dale Hopson

At left:
More therapy via sketchbook:

This picture was drawn thirty years ago during my well-paid, albeit troubled and short-lived, tenure as a "*Playboy* regular."

In "Barefootz Variations," a cathartic stream-of-consciousness catalog of my many conflicts and anxieties surrounding art, ambition, and the meaning of "undergroundness" that I splashed across six pages of *Barefootz Funnies #3* in 1979, I (almost) "let it all hang out."

Almost—but not quite.

SURE, INGMAR BERGMAN'S **GREAT** AT MAKIN' LITTLE 'INGMAR BERGMAN MOVIES', BUT IF INGMAR BERGMAN'D GET OFF HIS ASS AND MAKE **'JAWS'** —THAT'S WHEN HE'D BE IN TH' **BIG** MONEY!

A 'PRO' DISCUSSES ART...

AND WHAT WOULD **YOU** LIKE FOR CHRISTMAS, HOWIE?

...A **SYNDICATED COMIC STRIP?**

...AN **ANIMATED FILM?**

...A **REGULAR SPOT IN PLAYBOY?**

NOT **ME**, SANTA... I WANT TO STAY **PURE!**

"Gravy on Gay" had made it clear that my sympathies lay with the Gay Liberation Movement, but that wasn't the same as unambiguously asserting that I was gay myself. Then in August of 1979 Denis Kitchen asked me if I would like to helm a new comic book title he hoped to launch soon, to be called *Gay Comix*.

I immediately realized that accepting his invitation would provide a perfect opportunity to finally complete my coming-out process—and to do it in a matter-of-fact, nonconfessional way while contributing to an exciting and worthwhile artistic venture.

*At right: an excerpt from Denis Kitchen's letter to me.*

On another note altogether, would you be interested in editing (and, presumably, contributing to) a gay-oriented comic book? It's the kind of issue-comic I'm aiming more for. And I think it's a viable prod...
(the great...

*Below: the opening paragraphs of my subsequent letter to cartoonists describing our plans for Gay Comix and soliciting contributions to its first issue (and coming out in the process).*

**Dear Artist:**

Denis Kitchen has invited me to edit an underground comic book relating to being a lesbian or gay male in today's world. The projected title of the book is simply GAY COMIX.

This letter is being mailed to Denis's entire mailing list of artists, straight and gay. If you are not gay yourself, you may help by passing it on to any of your cartooning friends who are.

Many gay artists have never included the gay facets of their lifestyle in their published work, whether from fear of ostracism on a personal level, possible negative reaction from fans, or the chance that homophobia among editors or publishers could result in long-range career damage. As a gay artist myself, I have shared those fears...

To Denis's and my delight, underground veterans like Mary Wings, Roberta Gregory, and Lee Marrs, all of whom had already introduced lesbianism and bisexuality into their own comix, responded with enthusiasm to my invitation. Rand Holmes, the Canadian creator of *Harold Hedd Comix*, whose title character slept with babes aplenty but had also hopped cheerily into bed with a hunk at least once, volunteered to contribute cover art. Obviously the time was right for *Gay Comix* and a new career chapter was beginning for me.

What caught me by surprise once I jettisoned my last vestiges of heterosexual privilege and began spilling my gay inner life onto paper, was the boost it can give to an artist's creativity to have a lifetime's worth of secrets and fears flushed out of his or her brain with one single jolt of honesty.

# My Strips from Gay Comix 1980-90

Lesbians and Gay Men Put It On Paper!

GAY comix

I'VE BEEN STANDING BY TOO LONG WITHOUT **COMMITTING** MY **ART** TO THE STRUGGLE!

# BILLY GOES OUT

1980 in New York City: Before the epidemic had reared its head

by HOWARD CRUSE

Published in *Gay Comix #1*

SIGH!! DIS GUY'S MY FANTASY!
Thanks for some great times, World! Love, Billy
I HATE TO PHONE YOU SO LATE, BILLY, BUT YOUR COUSIN JUST CALLED! UNCLE STUART DIED THIS AFTERNOON...
GEE, MOM, I'M SORRY TO HEAR THAT! DID HE EVER COME OUT OF THE COMA?
BEING DEAD ISN'T THAT DIFFERENT FROM BEING ALIVE, NEPHEW...YOU JUST DECAY FASTER!
SO LONG, UNCLE STUART
NO, BUT THERE DIDN'T SEEM TO BE ANY PAIN AT THE END...
I'LL WRITE A NOTE TO AUNT MO TOMORROW!
I WISH I COULD GET AWAY FOR THE FUNERAL, BUT...
IF YOU'RE GOING TO GET AHEAD IN THIS WORLD, BILLY, YOU'VE GOT TO KEEP THIS 'QUEER' STUFF UNDER WRAPS!
AND FOR GOD'S SAKE, DON'T LET YOUR FOLKS FIND OUT!
HOW ARE YOU GETTING ALONG, SON? DID YOU GET WORD ON THE PROMOTION YET?
I EXPECT I'LL HEAR SOMETHING BY NEXT WEEK...
SO WE'VE GOT ANOTHER BACHELOR IN THE COMPANY -EH, WILLIAM? I'LL HAVE TO ALERT THE GIRLS IN THE STENO POOL ABOUT THAT SITUATION! CHUCKLE!
HA HA
YOU DIDN'T EVEN HAVE TO TELL ME, HONEY! ANYBODY'D KNOW THAT YOU AND BRAD ARE IN LOVE! I THINK IT'S TERRIFIC!
WHEW!! I WASN'T SURE HOW YOU'D FEEL ABOUT IT, JAN!
OH, BILLY... ARE YOU GOING TO JOIN THE GANG AT THE MUSEUM ON WEDNESDAY?
I'LL BE THERE!
WHERE'S ROFFO, MOM?
BILLY, HE GOT HIT BY A CAR WHILE YOU WERE PLAYING AT TOMMY'S HOUSE...
2

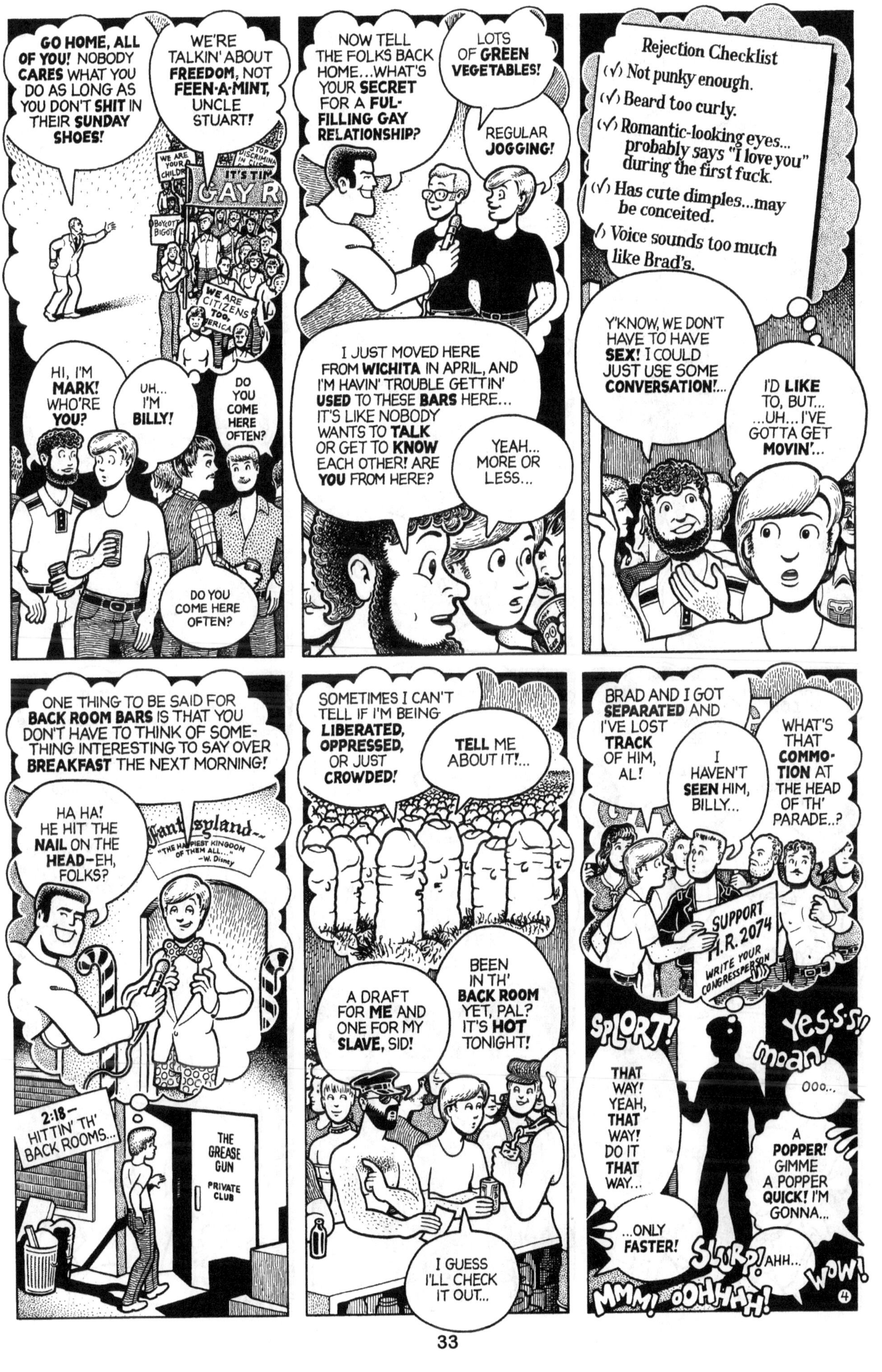

35

# JERRY MACK

©1981 by H. Cruse

MY NAME IS **JERRY MACK WYATT.** I'VE BEEN A MINISTER HERE IN IOWA SINCE 1964.

LET US PRAY...

MOST MORNINGS I EAT EARLY, BEFORE THE FAMILY IS UP. TODAY I WAS READING THE **PAPER** OVER MY **CORN FLAKES** AND A STORY TOOK MY MIND BACK TO **1958...**

HAPPY COW MILK

THE LORD HAS BLESSED ME WITH A **LARGE** AND **LOVING FAMILY!**

THE ARTICLE WAS ABOUT **EVAN BOND.**

HE'S **GROWN UP** NOW, BUT TO ME...HE'LL ALWAYS BE **SIXTEEN.**

EVAN USED TO COME OUT TO MY PLACE WHEN I LIVED IN **SPARROW CREEK,** A SMALL TOWN IN **ALABAMA.**

HOWDY, J.M...

EVAN'S DAD **OSCAR** HAD A **HARDWARE STORE** THERE. WHEN I MOVED INTO TOWN, HE TOOK AN **INTEREST** IN ME.

YOU CAN HAVE A JOB **HERE,** SON! YOUR **AUNT** DID MANY A FAVOR FOR **ME!**

OSCAR'S HARDWARE COMPANY

I WAS A **YOUNG MAN** AND DIDN'T KNOW WHAT I **WANTED** OUT OF LIFE.

JESUS WAS CALLING ME TO THE MINISTRY **EVEN THEN,** BUT I RESISTED.

I LIVED BY MYSELF IN A **FARMHOUSE** THAT MY AUNT LUCY LEFT TO MY FOLKS WHEN SHE DIED.

MY FOLKS WERE HAPPY TO LET ME **LIVE** THERE FOR **FREE,** SINCE THEY DIDN'T WANT TO LEAVE OUR HOME IN **GEORGIA.**

IN THE CELLAR THERE WAS AN OLD **MIMEO-GRAPH MACHINE** THAT AUNT LUCY HAD PICKED UP AT A **JUNK SHOP.**

I GOT THE IDEA OF USING IT TO PUBLISH A MONTHLY **LEAFLET** IN PRAISE OF THE **LORD!**

...AND Y'WANT **TEN REAMS** OF MIMEO PAPER?

PRINTING SUPPLIES

by **HOWARD CRUSE**

Published in *Gay Comix #2*

I CALLED MY PAPER 'SUBLIME ALLEGIANCE'...

IT'S A SWEET PAPER, JERRY MACK! WON'T YOU LET ME GIVE YOU A NICKEL FOR IT?

NO, MA'AM... IT'S FREE!

ALL OF THE LOCAL MERCHANTS BOUGHT ADS IN IT.

EVAN WAS WELL-KNOWN IN SPARROW CREEK BECAUSE OF HIS KNACK FOR DRAWING. HIS DAD KEPT AFTER ME TO USE THE YOUNGSTER'S ART IN MY PAPER. FINALLY I GAVE IT A TRY.

CAN YOU BELIEVE THIS KID'S NEVER HAD A LESSON IN HIS LIFE?

HE'S GOOD!

OSCAR'S HARDWARE COMPANY

IT WAS AMAZING HOW EVAN'S CARTOONS COULD LIVEN UP MY INSPIRATIONAL ESSAYS!

THE SIREN SONG OF SIN

Nothing is more ugly than sin, but nothing sings with a more sed...

EVAN AND I BECAME PALS!

HE USED TO COME OUT TO MY FARM TO DRAW HIS PICTURES ON THE BIG BLUE MIMEO STENCILS.

SAY, PICASSO...YOUR BUDDIES HAVE GOT THE FRANKS ON THE FIRE!

I'M ALMOST FINISHED...

SOMETIMES HE'D BRING ALONG HIS FRIENDS AND WE'D HAVE COOKOUTS.

THERE WAS A NICE CREEK NEARBY, PERFECT FOR AFTERNOON SWIMS.

DAVID'S 'IT'!

NOT FOR LONG!

EVAN'S PARENTS SAID I WAS A FINE SPIRITUAL INFLUENCE ON THEIR SON.

WHY, JERRY MACK, I'LL BET YOU NEVER COOK YOURSELF LIMA BEANS THIS GOOD OUT AT THAT OL' FARMHOUSE OF YOURS!

THEY HAD ME OVER FOR DINNER A LOT AND MADE A POINT OF INTRODUCING ME TO ATTRACTIVE YOUNG WOMEN IN THE TOWN.

I STILL COULD CRY WHEN I THINK HOW THEY CAME TO MISUNDERSTAND ME IN THE END.

IT ALL GREW OUT OF THE SIMPLE FRIENDSHIP THAT I FELT FOR EVAN. AS TIME WENT BY, THE FEELINGS GOT A LITTLE OUT OF HAND...

I THOUGHT YOU WERE GONNA WORK ON PAGE THREE!

MAKE ME!

I'D BE AROUND HIM AND FEEL GIDDY...SCARED... KIND OF LIKE I WAS RUNNING A FEVER...

DO YOU THINK I COULD LEARN TO DRAW WITH MY TOES, J.M.?

I'M SURE YOU COULD!

HE WAS JUST A KID, BUT YOU COULD SEE A MAN'S MUSCLES BUILDING UP ON THOSE SHOULDERS...

WATCH OUT, J.M....

HE LIKED TO SHOW OFF AND WRESTLE ME!

AM I GONNA HAVE TO TEACH YOU A LESSON, CHUM?

JUST TRY IT, JERRY MACK!

OH, I'D PIN HIM DOWN—I WAS SEVEN YEARS OLDER, AFTER ALL! BUT THAT KID COULD PUT UP A WOOLY FIGHT!

AFTER WE WRESTLED, I'D MAKE KOOL-AID AND PRAY TO GOD FOR HELP AGAINST THE TEMPTATIONS THAT WOULD CLUTCH AT MY SOUL...

②

WHEN I WOULD **DREAM** AT NIGHT, SATAN WOULD **TAKE OVER** MY FLESHLY DESIRES **ENTIRELY**...

CLEANSE MY **SOUL**, O JESUS...

...LIFT ME FROM MINE **ABYSS!!**

I WAS TORTURED WITH **SHAME** AT THE THINGS I WAS FEELING, BUT I DIDN'T DARE **SPEAK** OF THEM TO ANYONE.

I STUDIED THE **BIBLE**, TRIED TO GAIN **STRENGTH** AGAINST SATAN'S **ONSLAUGHTS**.

ONE EVENING EVAN CAME OUT TO THE FARM UNEXPECTEDLY.

I'M SORRY FOR NOT **'PHONING** FIRST...

IS SOMETHING **WRONG?**

HE HAD JUST THAT THURSDAY GOTTEN HIS **DRIVER'S LICENCE,** SO HE DROVE HIS **DADDY'S CAR.**

HE WAS UPSET AND CRYING BECAUSE HE HAD **BROKEN UP** WITH HIS **GIRLFRIEND.**

SHE WOULDN'T **LISTEN** TO ME! I WAS JUST TRYIN' TO **EXPLAIN** TO HER...

I TRIED TO **COMFORT** HIM AS BEST I COULD. ALL I DID WAS **HOLD** HIM CLOSE TO ME WHILE HE **SOBBED.** I DIDN'T MEAN ANY **HARM** BY IT.

MAYBE I SHOULDN'T HAVE **KISSED** HIM ON THE **FOREHEAD,** BUT HE DIDN'T SEEM TO **MIND.**

AS A MATTER OF FACT, BEFORE HE LEFT HE TOLD ME THAT I HAD **HELPED** HIM A **LOT.**

YOU'RE TH' BEST **FRIEND** I'VE EVER **HAD,** JERRY MACK!

I DIDN'T GET ANY SLEEP THAT NIGHT, AND NOT MUCH FOR THE NEXT WEEK-OR-SO!

THE NEXT TIME EVAN CAME OVER TO DRAW HIS CARTOONS, HE SAID THAT HE AND HIS GIRLFRIEND HAD **MADE UP** AND WERE **GOING STEADY** AGAIN!

**WE** PRAISED THE LORD TOGETHER!

LATER, WHEN HE WAS GONE, I WAS SEIZED WITH AN AWFUL **TREMBLING!** I KNEW I HAD TO TALK TO HIM SOME MORE...

I TELEPHONED HIM AT HIS HOME. HIS DAD ANSWERED.

H-HELLO, **OSCAR?** THIS IS **JERRY MACK!** MAY I SPEAK TO **EVAN?**

EVAN CAME TO THE PHONE. I ASKED HIM TO MEET ME AT A NEARBY **TRUCK STOP** IN AN HOUR. FOR SOME REASON, I WAS AFRAID FOR US TO BE BACK AT MY PLACE **ALONE**.

WHEN I SAW THE HEADLIGHTS OF HIS **CAR** PULLING IN, MY **HEART** STARTED **POUNDING**...

I STEPPED OUTSIDE. TWO CAR DOORS SLAMMED.

EVAN HADN'T COME. BUT HIS **FATHER** HAD ...AND HE HAD BROUGHT ALONG THE **LOCAL MINISTER**.

OSCAR WALKED UP TO ME AND STARTED **YELLING** AND **HITTING** ME IN THE **FACE**...

I BROUGHT THE **PREACHER** WITH ME 'CAUSE I KNEW HE WOULDN'T LET ME **KILL** YOU LIKE I'D **LIKE** TO, JERRY MACK!

*KRAK*

K-KILL ME??

THAT'S ALL YOU **DESERVE**, YOU **GODDAMNED QUEER!!**

PLEASE, OLLIE—NOT THE LORD'S NAME IN VAIN...

HE'D COMPLETELY **MISUNDERSTOOD** MY **MOTIVES** FOR PHONING EVAN.

I WANT YOU **OUT** OF THIS TOWN BY **TOMORROW** OR, BY GOD, YOUR **ASS'LL** BE SWINGIN' FROM THE **TOWN HALL** LAMP POST!

...PARDON TH' **LANGUAGE**, PREACHER!...

THAT'S ALL RIGHT, SON...

...AND DON'T YOU EVER **SPEAK** OR **WRITE A WORD** TO MY BOY **AGAIN!**

LET UP NOW, OSCAR...I THINK YOU'VE MADE YOUR **POINT!**

WHAT'S GOIN' ON, LILAH?

JUST SOME KINDA **FIGHT!** ...GO BACK INSIDE...

I APPRECIATE YOU COMIN' WITH ME, BROTHER RILEY...

ANYTIME, OSCAR! I KNOW THIS HAS BEEN UPSETTING FOR YOU...

THE WHOLE THING WAS A **NIGHTMARE!**

CONSIDERING HOW **LOW** I FELT AT THE TIME, IT'S A MIRACLE THAT I **EVER** GOT MY LIFE TOGETHER AGAIN...

*OW!*

I HAD TO MOVE AWAY FROM SPARROW CREEK, ALL RIGHT. THERE WAS NO WAY **AROUND** IT!

THE **WORST** OF IT WAS, I NEVER SAW EVAN AGAIN...NEVER HAD A CHANCE TO **EXPLAIN!**

BUT I **PRAYED** AND BEGGED GOD TO **FORGIVE** MY **UNWORTHINESS.** FINALLY HE GRANTED SOME **PEACE** TO MY **ACHING HEART.**

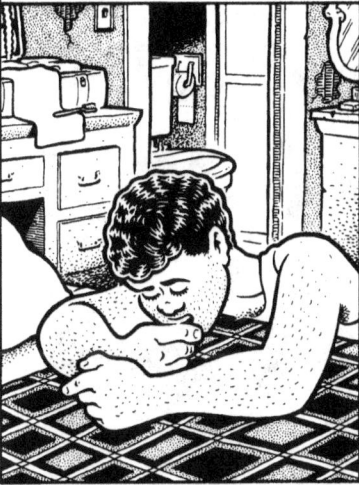

I DECIDED TO **SERVE** HIM FOR THE REST OF MY DAYS.

WHILE I WAS STUDYING AT THE **SEMINARY,** I GOT A FRIENDLY NOTE FROM **EVAN.**

HE WAS MARRIED. HE SENT ME A CUTE **SNAPSHOT** OF HIS **LITTLE GIRL.**

I MARRIED, TOO. I MET MY **SHIRLEY** THE FIRST YEAR OF MY MINISTRY.

AND ARE YOU A **MARRIED MAN,** REV. WYATT..?

SHE'S SEEN ME THROUGH SOME **ROUGH TIMES.** SHIRLEY'S A **TRUE SAINT.**

THE LORD HAS BLESSED US WITH A **LARGE** AND **LOVING** FAMILY.

TWO OF MY GIRLS ARE STUDYING TO BE **FOREIGN MISSIONARIES.**

WHAT STARTED ME OFF TODAY WAS SEEING THIS **ARTICLE** ABOUT **EVAN** IN THE MORNING PAPER. IT SEEMS HE LEFT HIS **WIFE** AND **DAUGHTER** SOME YEARS BACK.

HAPPY COW MILK

NOW HE'S PUBLISHING COMIC STRIPS ABOUT 'GAY LIBERATION'...

Changing
Gay Cartoonist Says 'Liberate Comic Strips!'

YES, THAT'S WHAT THEY **CALL** IT!

Crush

THEY PRINTED HIS PHOTOGRAPH AT THE TOP. HE'S AS HANDSOME AS **EVER.**

...Alabama-born Evan Bond says he's gay...
...are his characters.

HOW DID THE DEVIL EVER GET HOLD OF SUCH A **FINE YOUNG MAN?**

MY YOUNGEST SON TOM **REMINDS** ME OF EVAN SOMETIMES. HE'S **SPUNKY...CREATIVE**...SHOWS SOME DEFINITE **DRAWING TALENT**...

CORN FLAKES

IF HE EVER TOLD ME HE WAS A **QUEER,** I... I THINK I'D...

MORNIN', DAD!

the end...

OH, LORD — **FORGIVE** ME FOR THESE **THOUGHTS**...THESE **THOUGHTS**...

# I ALWAYS CRY AT MOVIES...

I GUESS THERE'S NOT MUCH LEFT TO **SAY** NOW, BABE...

MY STUFF'S IN THE CAR SO... HERE'S THE DOOR KEY.

THE MORE WE TALK, THE MORE WE **WOUND** EACH OTHER.

OH, DID I TELL YOU ABOUT THE JOB IN L.A.? I GOT THE WORD!

©1982 H. Cruse

I GUESS I WON'T **STARVE**, AND WHO KNOWS? (SIGH!) —MAYBE...

WELL... GOOD-BYE. AND LOOK, DON'T—

I ONLY HOPE YOU WON'T BE **BITTER.**

THE FOUR YEARS ARE PART OF **BOTH** OF US. THEY ALWAYS **WILL** BE.

ESPECIALLY **HOME MOVIES!**

# GETTING DOMESTIC

Published in *Gay Comix #2*

44

...SO I TOLD HIM, 'I'M SORRY, BUT I COULD **NEVER** FALL IN LOVE WITH A **PRESIDENT'S SON!**...'

## BACKSTORY

About Luke and Clark's opening repartee in
### "Dirty Old Lovers"

President Ronald Reagan's son Ron was widely rumored within gay activist circles during the 1980s to be secretly gay. No actual evidence that this is true has arisen since then, suggesting that some regrettable former-male-ballet-dancer-profiling may have been at work. It was an enjoyable rumor to indulge at the time, given the Reagan crowd's homophobic tenor overall, but in light of the younger Ron Reagan's subsequent emergence as a progressive ally who even hosts a show on the liberal Air America Radio, the impulse within activist circles to rib Ron over his one-time affinity for ballet slippers has been pretty much retired.

STORY BEGINS ON NEXT PAGE

**B**Y DAY, **CLARK STOBBER** IS MANAGER OF A FAST-GROWING CHAIN OF VIDEO SUPPLY OUTLETS...

How many units..?

$!

**A**ND PERHAPS YOU'VE HEARD OF **LUKE TEWBA**, AUTHOR OF A CRITICALLY ACCLAIMED BOOK ON HOLISTIC PODIATRY...

**C**LARK VOLUNTEERS HIS EXECUTIVE SKILLS TO NUMEROUS PUBLIC SERVICE GROUPS WITHIN THE GAY COMMUNITY...

We could set up a media center here...

...and fund it through the collective!

**L**UKE IS A THEORIST WHOSE PERCEPTIONS ARE REGULARLY SOUGHT BY GAYS INVOLVED IN EDUCATIONAL PROJECTS...

But you can't approach liberation with a disco mentality...

So true!

**A**S LONGTIME LOVERS AND PARTNERS IN GAY ACTIVISM, CLARK AND LUKE ARE WIDELY LAUDED FOR THEIR CONTRIBUTIONS...

CLAP CLAP CLAP CLAP CLAP

**I**N OTHER WORDS, BY DAY THESE MEN SERVE AS ADMIRABLE ROLE MODELS FOR GAY PEOPLE EVERYWHERE...

Good morning, role model!

Hi there, widely lauded activist!

**B**UT BY NIGHT, THEY STROLL **SHAMELESSLY** DOWN THE PUBLIC STREETS, AN **EMBARRASS-MENT** TO US ALL—THOSE...

# DIRTY OLD LOVERS
## by Howard Cruse

...SO I TOLD HIM, 'I'M SORRY, BUT I COULD **NEVER** FALL IN LOVE WITH A **PRESIDENT'S SON!**...'

'..BESIDES, I ALREADY **HAVE** A LOVER!'

YOU REALLY SHOULD'VE BROKEN THE NEWS TO HIM BEFORE HE GOT HIS **TROUSER KNEES** ALL **MUDDY!**

©1982 by H. Cruse.

**T**HANK GOD **MOST** GAYS AREN'T LIKE **THEM!!**

Published in *Gay Comix #3*

**Panel 1:**
DID I GET THE **DATE** RIGHT? MY NAME IS **STEW BONSKI!** YOU AND YOUR LOVER SPOKE TO OUR **GAY EMOTIONAL HEALTH RAP GROUP** LAST MONTH!

AND YOU REMEMBERED THAT **TODAY** IS OUR **ANNIVERSARY!** YOU'RE SO **RETENTIVE!**

**Panel 2:**
YOU AND MISTER TEWBA WERE SO **INSPIRATIONAL!** I'D HAD A LOT OF **CONFUSION** AROUND THE ISSUE OF SUSTAINING **LONG-TERM RELATIONSHIPS,** AND YOU TWO CLEARED IT RIGHT **UP!**

HOW NICE THAT OUR WISDOM TOOK **ROOT!**

SMACK!

**Panel 3:**
IT BLOWS MY **MIND** TO THINK THAT YOU GUYS HAVE BEEN TOGETHER FOR **SO MANY YEARS...**

TIME DOES **FLY!**

THANKS FOR **WAITING,** CLARK!

**Panel 4:**
I'VE BEEN **DYING** TO BUY THIS **SUMMER FROCK** FOR **WEEKS,** BUT I COULD NEVER GET HERE DURING **BUSINESS HOURS!** DO YOU **LIKE** IT?...

**Panel 5:**
Y-YOU'RE WEARING A...

UH-OH! I THINK YOU'VE OPENED UP A **FRESH AREA** OF **EMOTIONAL CONFUSION** FOR STEWART HERE, LUKE!

I DIDN'T **MEAN** TO...

**Panel 6:**
WELL, NO HARM DONE! JUST BE SURE TO CHECK IN AT NEXT MONTH'S **RAP GROUP,** STEW...I HEAR THE SPEAKER IS **INEZ BOUQUET,** FAMOUS **DRAG CELLIST!** SHE'LL CLEAR UP YOUR CONFLICTS IN A JIFFY!

Pat Pat!

I CAN **PERSONALLY** VOUCH FOR INEZ...WE WERE IN THE **MARINES** TOGETHER!

**Panel 7:**
THESE YOUNGSTERS AND THEIR **CONFLICTS!**

SHALL WE STOP IN FOR A **BEER** AT 'BEAU'S' AND RAISE A **TOAST** TO OUR **LIVER SPOTS?**

BEAU'S

**Panel 8:**
WE'RE DRAWING **STARES,** LUKE!

IT'S MY **FROCK,** I'LL BET! YOU KNOW HOW THESE 'MACHISMO QUEENS' ARE- IF A PIECE OF LADIES' WEAR ISN'T TRIMMED IN **LEATHER,** THEY WON'T EVEN **TRY** IT ON!

**Panel 9:**
ARE YOU LOOKING AT ME **ASKANCE,** YOUNG MAN, OR IS IT MERELY **LUST?** DON'T YOU THINK I'M **CHIC?** ARE YOU PREJUDICED AGAINST **FLORAL PATTERNS?** WHAT'S YOUR **ASTROLOGICAL SIGN?**...

STATE UNIVERSITY

NOT FUNNY.
NOT FUNNY...
NOT FUNNY!

SNAP!
CRACKLE!
POP!

THE ARTIST EMBARKS
ON A PERILOUS
VOYAGE...

## BACKSTORY

### About "Safe Sex"

By the time I hunkered down to draw my own contribution to *Gay Comix* #4, it was clear that AIDS would have to be addressed in some way within the issue's pages. The horror was too present in LGBT people's minds to be ignored.

By then two years had passed since the epidemic was first thrust into our consciousness by an article asserting that 47 gay men had suddenly been diagnosed with a "rare cancer." Bit by bit, the role of compromised immune systems was discovered as the afflictions besetting gay men expanded far beyond the cancers that first set off alarm bells. The death toll was soon skyrocketing, and the disease nomenclature mutated from "gay cancer" to GRID (for Gay-Related Immune Deficiency), finally becoming the non-gay-specific diagnosis AIDS (Acquired Immune-Deficiency Syndrome), in recognition of the fact that populations other than gay men were also vulnerable.

So some acknowledgment of AIDS had to appear in *Gay Comix*, but that didn't make it ideal fodder for a comic strip. I contemplated a narrative depicting the course of some comic strip character's illness, but anything I came up with began accumulating weepy disease-of-the-week tropes by page two. The last thing I wanted to do was trivialize the real-world suffering being endured by a growing portion of the *Gay Comix* readership by sentimentalizing it.

As you can see from the pages that follow, I opted in the end for a different tactic, building a comic strip around the psychic chaos that we LGBT folks were all going through, whether or not we were individually infected with HIV (then referred to as HTLV-3). I tried to amplify our collective distress with page layouts that were as jagged as our nerves were back then as we cared for our friends, surveyed our bodies for KS lesions, and looked over our shoulders for signs that quarantine camps were under construction.

Oh, yes—and as we tried to keep our senses of humor alive.

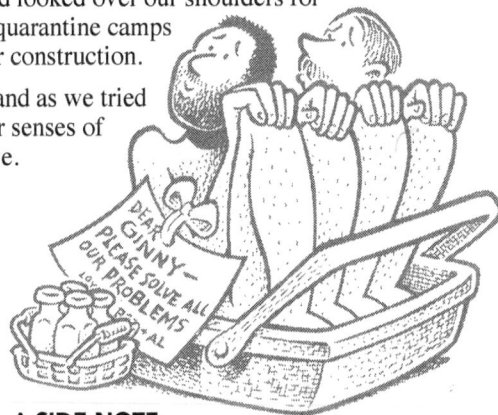

DEAR GINNY—
PLEASE SOLVE ALL
OUR PROBLEMS

**A SIDE NOTE:**

The "Ginny" into whose care the gay men are offering themselves on the fourth page of "Safe Sex" is Virginia Apuzzo, who was the Executive Director of what was then called the National Gay Task Force and a reliably eloquent advocate for LGBT liberation.

STORY BEGINS
ON NEXT PAGE

# Ready or not, here it comes...

©1983 H. Cruse

NOT FUNNY.
*NOT FUNNY...*
**NOT FUNNY!**

SNAP! CRACKLE! POP!

YOWCH!

THE ARTIST EMBARKS ON A PERILOUS VOYAGE...

JUST REDUCED ANXIETY

IT'S A GREAT YEAR TO STAY ALIVE.

FRANKLY, I'VE NEVER BEEN PROUDER OF THE GAY AND LESBIAN COMMUNITY...

I HAVEN'T BEEN SO SCARED OF SEX SINCE I WAS A TEEN!

HE STARTED GETTING SO THIN...

WHAT DID THEY SAY AT THE CLINIC?

EVEN MY MOM WAS READY TO PICKET AFTER SHE READ PAT BUCHANAN'S HOMO-PHOBIC SHIT!

AND THE NURSES WANTED TO LEAVE HIS MEALS OUT IN THE HALL.

GOD!

KAPOSI'S SARCOMA

HELL, MORE LESBIANS HAVE COME TO VISIT ME THAN GAY MEN...

HEY NO

CAN A BABY GET IT?

POLITICALLY, THEY'VE GOT A TIGER BY THE TAIL...

YOU'RE **NOT ALLOWED** IN HERE...THE **DOCTORS** ARE **WORKING!**

HOW INTRUSIVE!

MY LIFESTYLE EVERYTHING'S A THEORY.

AT THE CANDLELIGHT VIGIL...

THEY ASKED HIM NOT TO COME TO HIS GODCHILD'S CHRISTENING...

I JUST CAN'T TAKE ANOTHER FUNERAL THIS YEAR.

BUT I'M SCARED TO COME OUT OF THE CLOSET...

WHAT LAST WORDS? HE COULDN'T SPEAK!

FROM BLOOD TRANSFUSIONS???

LOVE

NO ADMI

GAY LOVE — IN BLOOM AS ALWAYS...

YESTERDAY I PHONED MY FOLKS TO TELL THEM ALL ABOUT **YOU!**

AND THIS MORNING I WROTE **MY** FOLKS A LETTER TO TELL THEM ALL ABOUT **YOU!**

WHILE AT THE TWILIGHT ZONE BRANCH OF THE BUENO BONER BATHS...

IT'S REALLY **WEIRD!**...

...I'VE WATCHED **EIGHTY-THREE MEN** GO INTO THAT STEAM ROOM IN THE LAST HOUR...

...AND **NOT A ONE HAS COME BACK OUT!!!**

by **Howard Cruse** ...from NEW YORK CITY in the Summer of '83

①

52

Published in *Gay Comix #4*

THE TRIP DOWNTOWN AIN'T WHAT IT USED TO BE!

"Ask not for whom the bell tolls..."

FEAR OF THE KISS THAT KILLS...

WELL, WELL, WELL...WE'VE BEEN LOOKING FOR AN OPPORTUNITY TO BRING YOU BOYS AROUND TO OUR WAY OF THINKING...

(CHOMP! CHOMP!) MAKES SENSE TO ME!!

'UNCLE!' 'UNCLE!' GARGH...

GET YOUR SHIT TOGETHER, YOU DODOS!!

New York Navel

FOLKS IN CANDYLAND LIKE THEIR MORALS SIMPLE!

NAUGHTY NASTY MENS GET A.I.D.S.

A CONCERNED GAY PRESS ABANDONS UNDERSTATEMENT!

JUDY GARLAND —HER LIFE AND HER MASCARA

'What do I care how much it may storm...'

SAINTS PRESERVE US!!

IT JUST HADDA BE A SEXUALLY-TRANSMITTED DISEASE, DIDN'T IT?

YEH...

'...CAN YA IMAGINE TH' HYSTERIA IF IT TURNED OUT THAT PEOPLE CAUGHT IT FROM BIBLES...??'

YES, IT'S FORCED ME TO REEVALUATE MY WHOLE LIFE-STYLE!

DEPT. OF SANITATION

Shrill Street News FINAL
GOD'S WRATH STRIKES DOW SELF-RIGHTEC HYPOCRITES

IT'S FUNNY HOW WE HUMAN BEINGS CAN BE SO AFRAID OF OUR GENITALS!

WE'RE GOING TO TELL SOMEBODY WHAT YOU'D LIKE TO DO WITH US...

N-NO... PLEASE!!

②

NOW BONNIE AND I HAVE ALWAYS DUG MONOGAMY, BUT I DON'T THINK WE'D WANT TO BE TERRORIZED INTO IT!
DEFINITELY UNSEXY!
JANINE AND BONNIE RAP ABOUT ROMANCE
ARRIVING FROM HAITI...
HEY!
PRESUMED SICK UNTIL PROVEN WELL
IN DEFIANCE OF MEDICAL WARNINGS AND REASONABLE PRUDENCE, TWO HOMOSEXUALS EXCHANGE BODY FLUIDS IN A DARK ALLEY...
BEEN WATCHING A LOT OF T.V. NEWS RECENTLY, MOM?
NEGOTIATIONS FOR A HOT DATE GET COMPLICATED...
is stipulated by this addition, by his signatur the party of the first part guarantees that, due to health considerations, there shall transpire in the course of the evening in question no sucking, fucking, kissing or
However, nothing in this contract should be interpreted as prohibiting rubbing, scrubbing, provocative massage techniques, fantasy garb or extended bouts of heavy breathing.
ZZZ...
CAN I BRING ALONG MY JOHN TRAVOLTA POSTER?
GOOD NEWS FOR FOOT-FETISHISTS:
NO MUCOUS MEMBRANES!
DID YOU HEAR ABOUT—?
DID YOU HEAR ABOUT—?
SUE SAID THAT MARTIN HAS A FRIEND WHO—
LET'S TALK TERMINOLOGY...
I AM A PERSON WITH AIDS!
I AM NOT AN 'AIDS VICTIM!'
I AM NOT AN 'AIDS PATIENT!'
PRESS
PRESS
YES, AND WHEN EXACTLY DID YOU CATCH THE 'GAY PLAGUE'..?
3

WAKE UP... WAKE UP... YOU'RE HAVING A NIGHTMARE!

NOW DON'T MIND ME!!

...BUT WHAT MIGHT I BE INCUBATING..?

LISTEN, THERE'S NOTHING TO WORRY ABOUT!

OH...UH— I THOUGHT THERE WAS...

ANXIETY INVADES THE HALLS OF ONAN...

WAIT A MINUTE... WHAT'S THAT WEIRD BLEMISH ON TH' BLOND GUY'S ANKLE?

STEAMY STUDS

BUTCH BARBERS

BEEN FEELING VERY HEALTHY LATELY, THANKS!

WELL, I FOR ONE FIND ALL THIS AIDS TALK DEPRESSING!

I AGREE! LET'S TALK ABOUT...

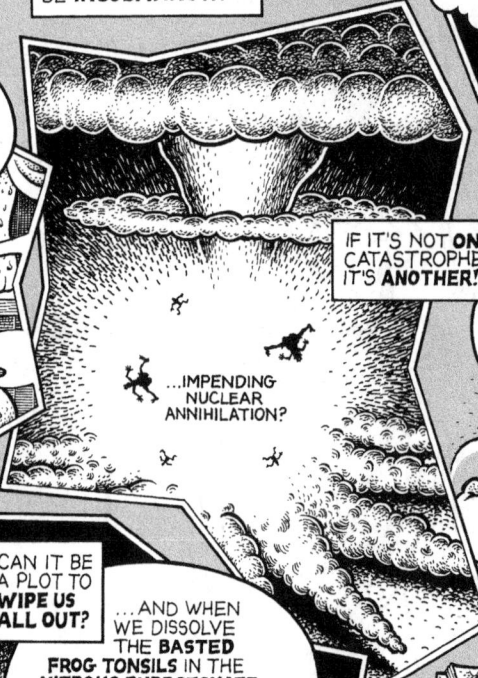

...IMPENDING NUCLEAR ANNIHILATION?

IF IT'S NOT ONE CATASTROPHE, IT'S ANOTHER!

HEY, MAUDE, EL SALVADOR JUST PASSED DIOXIN ON THE 'ANXIETY HIT PARADE!'

JUNIOR WANTS TO KNOW IF AIDS IS STILL ON THE CHARTS!

BUT THE PREZ IS ON TOP OF THINGS!

LIKE NANCY SAYS, WE'VE GOTTA STAY 'SEX-POSITIVE,' FOLKS!

SO KEEP ON BOOGEY-ING!!

CAN IT BE A PLOT TO WIPE US ALL OUT?

...AND WHEN WE DISSOLVE THE BASTED FROG TONSILS IN THE NITROUS BURBOTOXATE AND PIPE THE RESULTANT FUMES INTO CAREFULLY SELECTED BETTE MIDLER CONCERTS...

NYUK NYUK NYUK

CIA CENTRAL INTELLIGENCE AGENCY PURCHASE ORDER

TOP SECRET SUPER COVERT DIRTY BIZNESS!! SO DON'T TELL NOBODY Y'HEAR?

WE MUST BE EVER VIGILANT!

HOLD ON! (GLUB!) THAT BOTTLE OF PERRIER MAY BE TAINTED!!

57

Published in *Gay Comix #5*

Panel 1:
THIS IS MY NEW LOVER WESLEY! HE'S AN ARIES! THEY'RE VERY POETIC!

HOW NICE!

Panel 2:
WESLEY AND I ARE CELEBRATING OUR FIRST TWO WEEKS TOGETHER! WE'RE UNIMAGINABLY HAPPY—AND WE HAVEN'T FOUGHT ONCE!

Panel 3:
WHERE SHOULD WE GO ON OUR VACATION THIS YEAR, WESLEY? YOU'RE RIGHT...SAINT-TROPEZ WOULD BE PERFECT!

TRAVEL

Panel 4:
WESLEY AND I HAVE A WONDERFUL LOVE LIFE! FOR THE FIRST TIME IN MY LIFE I'M TRULY FULFILLED!

Panel 5:
OH, WESLEY, YOU'RE SO HOT! OH, GOD!!—I'M COMING! Gasp...

Panel 6:
DID YOU ENJOY YOUR CEREAL, WESLEY? BOY, WERE YOU SEXY LAST NIGHT! NEXT LET'S GET DRESSED AND GO TO THE GALLERY OPENING TOGETHER!

Panel 7:
I ENJOY LOOKING AT ART SO MUCH MORE SINCE I'VE BEEN WITH WESLEY! I'VE ALWAYS BEEN LIMITED BY MY INTELLECTUALISM, BUT WESLEY TAPS INTO THE REAL SPIRITUAL UNDER-CURRENTS...

ARE YOU TWO GOING TO THE MARCH ON SUNDAY?

Panel 8:
GAY RIGHTS NOW! GAY RIGHTS NOW!

WE ARE EVERYWHERE

GAY IS GREAT

WE'RE PROUD OF OUR BEAUTIFUL GAY RELATIONSHIP

Panel 9:
UNEXPECTEDLY, IN THE DARKNESS ONE NIGHT, WESLEY SPEAKS...

SOMETIMES I DON'T THINK YOU REALIZE THAT I'M MORE THAN JUST A DOLL, DEXTER!

ZZZ... !? HUH??

Y'KNOW, I HAVE **NEEDS** THAT ARE **ENTIRELY** INDEPENDENT OF **YOURS!** I FIND IT **TELLING** THAT YOU'VE NEVER EVEN **ASKED** ME ABOUT MY **CAREER GOALS!**

UH... I DIDN'T KNOW YOU COULD **TALK!**

THERE'S A **STIFLING** ASPECT TO ALL THIS **TOGETHERNESS** OF OURS! MAYBE A LITTLE **DISTANCE** IS CALLED FOR! AND WE HAVE SOME DIFFERENCES IN **BASIC VALUES** TO **IRON OUT!** THEN THERE'S THE FACT THAT I'M NOT FINDING YOU AS **HOT** AS I DID INITIALLY...

BUT—!?

SOONER OR LATER WE'RE GOING TO HAVE TO DEAL WITH THE PROS AND CONS OF **OUTSIDE SEX!** BUT AN EVEN **SUBTLER** ISSUE REVOLVES AROUND OUR **HOUSEKEEPING** ROLES...

**HEY!** I DON'T REMEMBER TH' CATALOG MENTIONIN' ANY OF **THIS** SHIT!

I ORDERED **AFFECTION**—NOT **COMPLICATIONS!**

BRP!

BONK!

**H**OW CRUELLY LOVE CAN END.

MAYBE IF I ORDER **ANOTHER** ONE, IT'LL ALL WORK OUT **BETTER!**

WE'RE GOING TO **OZ** TO SEE THE **WIZARD!** HE'S GOING TO SEND ME BACK TO **KANSAS**...

...AND GIVE ME A **BRAIN!**

...AND GIVE ME A **HEART!**

...AND GIVE ME SOME **COURAGE!**

GEE... DO YOU THINK THE WIZARD COULD FIND ME A **LOVER??**

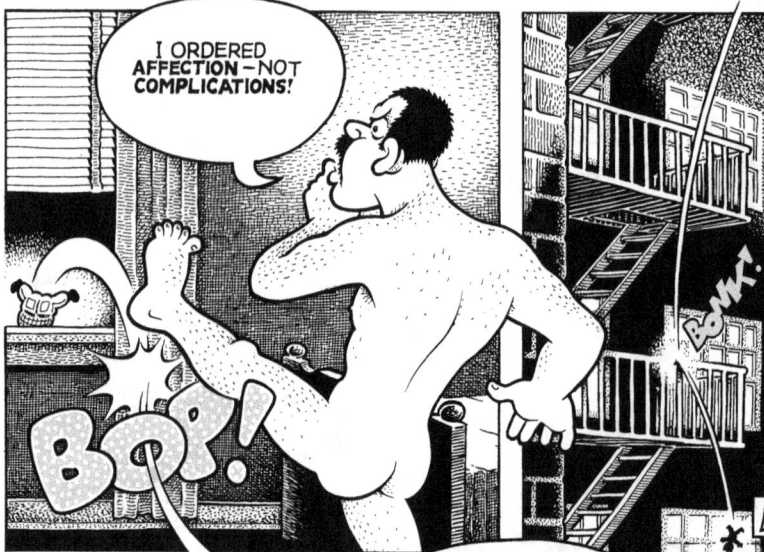

**C**OULD BE, DEXTER! AFTER ALL, THE MANUFACTURER GUARANTEES THAT **NO TWO CLONES** ARE **EXACTLY ALIKE!**

"**T**HANK GOD FOR THE GRACE OF **FANTASY!**" SIGHS THE CABBAGE PATCH CLONE.

The end

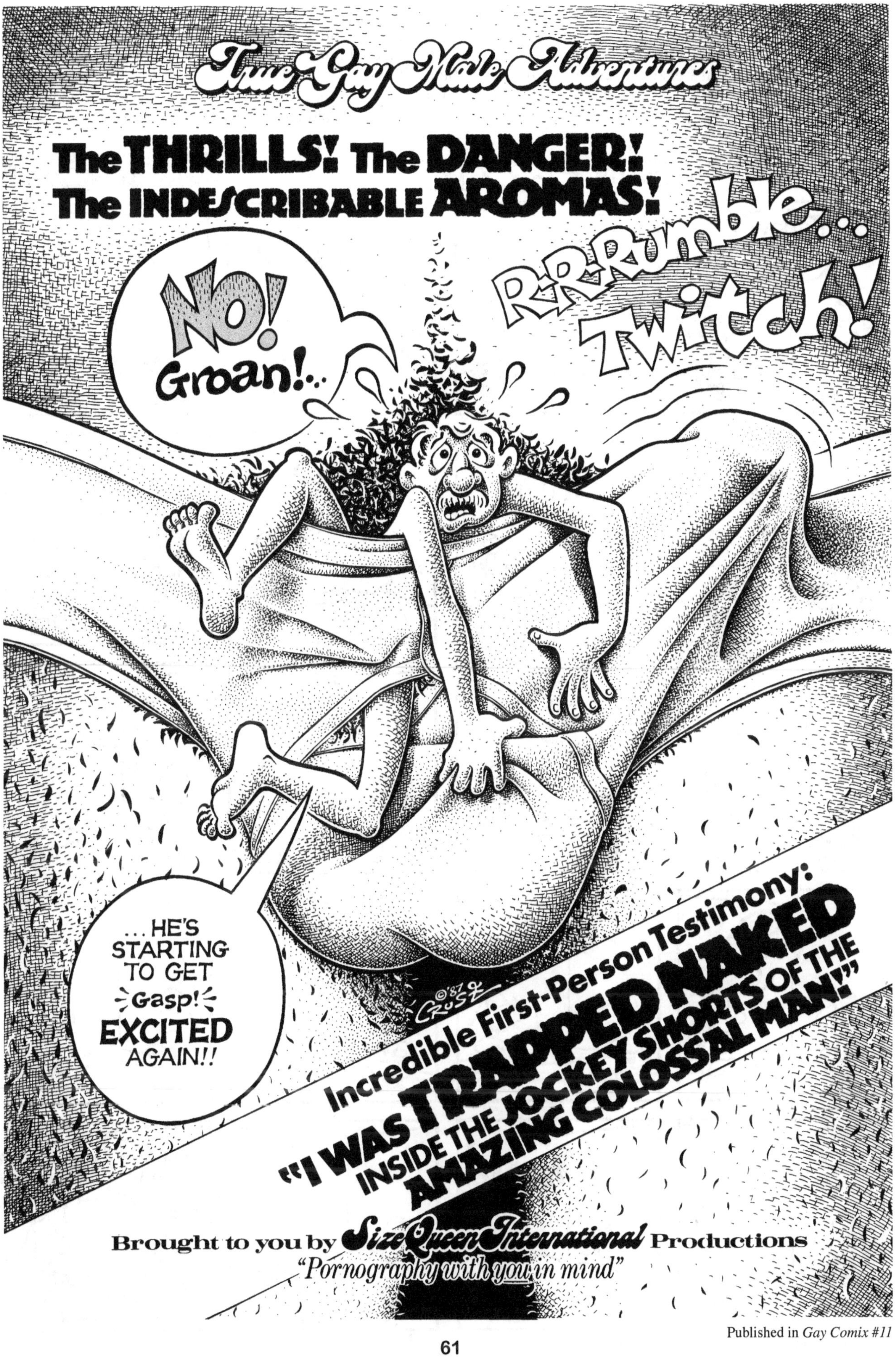


Published in *Gay Comix #11*

For the benefit of those who have never crossed paths with the weekly comic strip *Life in Hell*, created by cartoonist Matt Groening before television's *The Simpson* vaulted him into a new level of fame and fortune: the strip below is a spoof of Akbar and Jeff, recurring look-alike characters in the series and the most improbable representatives of gay coupledom ever to venture into public wearing matching Turkish headwear.

GAY DORKS IN FEZZES                by CRUSE

The village VOICE

VOL. XXX NO. 27   THE WEEKLY NEWSPAPER OF NEW YORK   JULY 2, 1985   $1.00

Talking Heads Start Making Sense
By James Nold Jr. (P. 77)

# GAY LIFE
## Trials of the Tribe

RICHARD GOLDSTEIN:
LARRY KRAMER'S COLD HEART

CINDY PATTON:
BRAVE NEW LESBIANS

ARMISTEAD MAUPIN:
TALKING WITH SHERWOOD

and More (P. 12)

Search and Destroy
Greg Tate on the New York 8+ (P. 31)

# Topical Strips
## 1983-93

**F**or a few years after *Gay Comix* called attention to my sexual orientation and demonstrated my willingness to invoke it publicly, I became the go-to guy for a few publications (principally New York City's *Village Voice*, but there were occasional others) when they were looking for an insider's outlook on LGBT topics of the day that could be expressed in the easily digested and generally reader-friendly comic strip format.

**T**he most gratifying aspect of such opportunities for spouting off was that,

when I was summoned to perform, I was promised page space for expressing my own attitudes in my own way, with no requirement that editors be shown where I was heading until I showed up at the office on deadline day with my finished artwork in hand.

**I**t takes a rare level of trust on the part of editors and art directors to work that way—a trust that was in the *Voice*'s case refreshingly in the spirit that made working in underground comix so fulfilling.

### About **"Sometimes I Get So Mad"**

Although readers of underground comix learned definitively that I am gay when *Gay Comix* was launched in 1980, it took the publication of "Sometimes I Get So Mad" in the *Village Voice* the following year to complete my emergence from the closet in the wider world.

I had lingering fears as that issue of the *Voice* hit the stands that some of my mainstream illustration clients might be spooked by my revelation and back away from hiring me. But the only client that bailed out on me was *Playboy*, and *Playboy* and I had never been that great a match.

# SOMETIMES I GET SO MAD...

### by HOWARD CRUSE

**Panel 1:**

HA HA! WELL, FOLKS, YOU'VE GOTTA KEEP YOUR SENSE OF **PERSPECTIVE!**..

THE OUTER ME

THE **BASTARDS!** I'LL **KILL** 'EM!

THE INNER ME

**Panel 2:**

**S**OMETIMES I GET SO MAD, IT'S NOT FUNNY!

HAVE YOU GOT THAT **SQUIRREL** TAMED YET, MR. MORRIS?

**JUST** ABOUT! SHE'LL COME RIGHT UP TO ME FOR A **SNACK**...

**Y**OU'D NEVER KNOW IT, THOUGH, WATCHING ME STROLL BY WITH MY MORNING GROCERIES.

**Panel 3:**

**I** TRY TO DRAW COMIC STRIPS ABOUT MY FEELINGS, BUT THEY COME OUT INCOHERENT!

SPUTTER!

GRUMBLE!

SNARL!

**Panel 4:**

Well, if God had wanted people to be **homosexuals**, Mike, he would've started with **Adam** and **Bruce!**

WHY DON'T YOU JUST TURN IT **OFF**, HOWIE? THAT STUFF ONLY **UPSETS** YOU!

GRRR...

**Panel 5:**

**M**Y THERAPIST WANTS TO GET THROUGH TO THE CORE...

WHAT **IS** IT EXACTLY THAT YOU **FEAR** THE **MOST?**

THESE **RELIGIOUS FANATICS** ARE GOING TO REDUCE MY LIFE TO **CHAOS!!**

**Panel 6:**

**I** HAVE DREAMS ABOUT GIANT TIDAL WAVES SUDDENLY ENGULFING ME ON THE STREET...

WAIT! THIS ISN'T **FAIR!**...

**Panel 7:**

**I** REMEMBER THE HELL OF BEING AN EMERGING GAY TEENAGER, TRYING TO FIGURE OUT WHAT WAS GOING ON INSIDE OF ME FROM THE SKIMPY AND BIGOTED LITERATURE OF THE TIME...

OBOY! NOW I CAN GET A **REAL MEDICAL OPINION!**

POCKET GUIDE TO LOATHSOME DISEASES BY DR. POMPOUS J. FRAUDQUACK

Devotional Fatuosity Press

Jesus's Favorite Recipes

**Panel 8:**

**A**ND I STARE AT THE FACES IN THE MILLING CROWDS, WONDERING...

WHO **ARE** THEY?? WHO ARE THE PEOPLE THAT WANT TO **BRING BACK** THAT **MISERY?**

**Panel 9:**

**P**UNKS WERE OUT AGAIN LAST NIGHT, HUNTING FOR 'QUEERS' TO BASH! I WONDER WHEN MY NUMBER WILL COME UP...

Published in *The Village Voice*

A 'MORAL MAJORITY' HONCHO IN CALIFORNIA THINKS I SHOULD BE EXECUTED!

LET'S MAKE THIS QUICK, FAGGOT! WE GOT A FEW MILLION IN LINE AFTER YOU!

© 1981 by H. Cruse

I USED TO GET BY NICELY ON THE COSMIC PLANE, BUT STATIC FROM THE MATERIAL WORLD BEGAN TO DISRUPT MY MANTRAS...

♪ HARE GUMBO OMMMM... ♪

A MINIMAL JAIL SENTENCE WAS HANDED DOWN TODAY TO THE CONVICTED MURDERER OF A PROMINENT GAY PUBLIC OFFICIAL IN SAN FRANCISCO. FORMER POLICE OFFICER... RIOTS ENSUED...

RICH CELEBRITIES WHO ARE GAY KEEP THE GAY MOVEMENT AT A SAFE DISTANCE...

NEW LAFF-RIOT SEQUEL FOR THE EIGHTIES "THE BOYS IN THE BAND GET STOMPED"

STOP PROFITS FROM ANTI-GAY VIOLENCE

PROTEST GAY STEREOTYPES IN FILMS

MY HEART IS WITH THEM, BUT THEY'RE GOING TOO FAR!

I'D LOVE TO HELP, BUT MY CAREER MIGHT SUFFER!

THE GAY COUPLE DOWNSTAIRS FLEES TO FIRE ISLAND ON GAY PRIDE SUNDAY...

I CAN'T DEAL WITH THOSE MARCHES AND SPEECHES! EVERYBODY'S SO INTENSE!

THE WHOLE 'GAY RIGHTS' BUSINESS TURNS ME OFF ANYWAY! WHO NEEDS MORE RIGHTS? I GET MORE SEX THAN I NEED, AS IT IS!

THE YOUNG MINISTER AT MY DOOR, FRESH FROM SEMINARY, SMILES AS HE INFORMS ME:

NOTHING PERSONAL FRIEND, BUT THE BIBLE SAYS THAT YOUR LOVE IS AN ABOMINATION BEFORE GOD!

SOMEWHERE OUT THERE, BENIGHTED SCHOOLS MANUFACTURE THEM BY THE THOUSANDS!

AND THE FAG JOKES ROLL ON...

SO THE FAGGOT SAYS TO THE TRUCK DRIVER, 'I MAY BE A PANTHY, BUT I'M NO FWOOT!'

HAR HAR!

BUMP!

ENTHUSIASTIC AUDIENCES LAP UP DEMAGOGUERY LIKE MILK...

...AND THE VOICE OF THE LORD HAS COMMANDED US TO HALT THE MARCH OF UNHOLY PERVERTS ON THE SACRED BASTIONS OF OUR CHRISTIAN FAMILY LIFE!

Amen!

Bring back Morality!

Ya-Hoo!

MY LOVER MUSES ABOUT AN EVENTUAL RELOCATION TO SWITZERLAND...

THEY HAVE COMIC BOOKS OVER THERE! DONALD DUCK IS HUGE IN SWITZERLAND!

I DON'T WANT TO BE A REFUGEE! I WANT TO LIVE IN AMERICA AND EAT BIG MACS AND HAVE MY RIGHTS AS A TAX-PAYING CITIZEN!!

IN MY FANTASIES, I HEROICALLY DEMOLISH THE SICK ARGUMENTS OF THE GUILT-MONGERS WITH MY CLEAR-HEADED WIT...

...AND THIS IS WHAT YOU CALL 'CHRISTIAN LOVE'? COME, COME, GENTLEMEN!

CLAP CLAP CLAP CLAP CLAP CLAP CLAP

...BUT IN REALITY, I FLAIL INEFFECTUALLY AT DISEMBODIED ADVERSARIES ON TV SCREENS AND IN SUPERMARKET TABLOIDS...

SIN! UN-NATURAL! PERVERSION

BUT YOU'RE WRONG...

THAT'S BULLSHIT!

THE NATIONAL DISGUSTING HOMOSEXUAL

THE FRUSTRATION OF RELENTLESS INJUSTICE AND SLANDER PROVOKES INTERIOR PAROXYSMS OF...

ALEEE!!

OF COURSE, I TRY NOT TO LET IT INTERFERE WITH MEETING MY DEADLINES!

HERE'S THE COMIC STRIP, SIR! I HOPE YOU LIKE IT!

RIGHT ON TIME, CRUSE! THE MARK OF A PRO!

the end

**The GAY in the STREET**
by Howard Cruse

LOOK! THERE'S ONE!

EXCUSE ME, SIR, BUT—THIS BEING GAY PRIDE WEEK—DO YOU HAVE ANY COMMENT ON THE FUTURE PROSPECTS FOR GAY PEOPLE?

BEAR IN MIND THAT WHATEVER YOU SAY WILL BE EDITED DOWN TO THREE SECONDS!

OMIGOD! THE WORLD IS WATCHING! I'VE GOTTA RISE TO THE OCCASION!

AHEM! WELL, UH, THESE ARE VERY COMPLICATED TIMES! WE'VE GOT THE FAR RIGHT AND THE "MORAL MAJORITY" EXPLOITING THE AIDS CRISIS... MUMBLE MUMBLE...SYSTEMIC HOMOPHOBIA... MUMBLE...APATHY AND POLITICAL ALIENATION AMONG CONSUMPTION-ORIENTED GAYS...MUMBLE...BICKERING GAY LEADERSHIP...MUMBLE... WHO KNOWS WHAT LIES AHEAD?..COULD BE BAD, COULD BE GOOD...IT'S HARD TO PULL TOGETHER IN A FEW WORDS...REALITY IS INEVITABLY DISTORTED!...

UH...COULD YOU PERHAPS BOIL SOME OF THAT DOWN?

YES, GETTING TO THE POINT HERE...DEEP PHILOSOPHICAL QUESTIONS HAVE BEEN RAISED BY RECENT EVENTS! THE FORMS AND ETHICS OF GAY SEXUAL EXPRESSION ARE BEING HOTLY DEBATED BY GAY THEORISTS THROUGHOUT THE LAND! WHO KNOWS WHAT COULD RESULT FROM ALL OF THAT THINKING? A LARGER BRAIN SIZE AMONG GAYS IS A DEFINITE EVOLUTIONARY POSSIBILITY!

JUST CONSIDER THE FASHION HEADGEAR RAMIFICATIONS OF THAT!!

Published in *The Village Voice*

AND SPEAKING OF **EVOLUTION**, THE COMING DECADES MAY CAST NEW LIGHT ON THE **ORIGINS** OF GAYNESS! FAR FROM CURRENTLY HELD THEORIES THAT WE SPRANG FROM **SPORES** PLANTED BY **ANCIENT EXTRA-TERRESTRIALS**, IT WILL EMERGE THAT WE ARE **MYSTICAL APPARITIONS** SENT BY **GOD** TO COMPLETE THE MISSION OF SPREADING **JOY** AND **LIGHT** WHICH THE LATE **JUDY GARLAND** LEFT TRAGICALLY UNFINISHED!

ON A LESS **ESOTERIC** FRONT, THE LEGALIZATION OF **GAY MARRIAGES** (FOR THOSE SO INCLINED) IS AN IDEA WHOSE TIME HAS COME...AND THE **BACKLOG** OF **ROMANTIC GAY MATRIMONIALISTS** IS SURE TO CHALLENGE THE NATION'S CAPACITY TO **SCHEDULE** AND **PERFORM** THE APPROPRIATE **CEREMONIES!**

WITH **CHURCHES, SYNAGOGUES, STADIUMS** AND **HAMBURGER CHAINS** FLOODED, OUR COUNTRY WILL TURN TO ITS POPULAR **TELEVISION PROGRAMS** AS VEHICLES FOR ABSORBING THE **OVERLOAD!**...

LESBIAN NUPTUALS WILL BE INCORPORATED SUBTLY INTO **CAGNEY & LACEY** PLOTS! GAY MALE COUPLES MAY GRAVITATE TOWARD THE CHEERY OPTIMISM OF **THE RICHARD SIMMONS SHOW**... OR, IF THEY'D RATHER GO FOR **BUTCH**, THEY CAN BE WED DURING THE COMMERCIAL BREAKS OF **STARSKY & HUTCH** RERUNS!

TERMINALLY **SERIOUS** GAYS WILL **ESCHEW FRIVOLITY** AND TAKE THEIR VOWS DURING TESTS OF THE **EMERGENCY BROADCAST SYSTEM!**

OF COURSE, WE CAN'T LET THE COMFORTS OF **DOMESTICITY** MAKE US FORGET THAT OUR MOVEMENT IS A CONTINUING ARM OF THE **SEXUAL REVOLUTION!** WE MUST NOT BECOME **TIMID!** WE MUST NOT TURN OUR BACKS ON OUR **RADICAL HISTORY!** WE MUST BOLDLY ASSERT OUR RIGHT TO **EXPRESS OUR-SELVES** AS HEALTHY **SEXUAL BEINGS!**

...LIKE FOR INSTANCE, I'M WEARING THIS FUNNY **PENIS HAT** THAT COULD HAVE GOTTEN ME **ARRESTED** IN THE **FIFTIES!**

SO YOU FORESEE THE YEARS AHEAD AS A PERIOD OF GAY MILITANCY?

MILITANCY! YOU WANNA HEAR ABOUT MILITANCY?? HOO BOY!..YOU DON'T KNOW FROM MILITANCY 'TIL YOU'VE SEEN THE MILITANCY THAT WE'RE GONNA COME UP WITH!

THE PIECES ARE ALREADY IN PLACE FOR OUR FINAL SURGE TOWARD JUSTICE!

FOR EXAMPLE (chuckle!)...DON'T LET JERRY FALWELL GET WIND OF THIS, BUT HUNDREDS OF FAMOUS, SECRETLY GAY STARS FROM TV AND HOLLYWOOD MEET EVERY THURSDAY AND COMPOSE PRO-HOMOSEXUAL MESSAGES WHICH ARE RECORDED BACKWARDS AND INSERTED INTO THE SOUNDTRACKS OF ALL OF OUR BEST-LOVED FAMILY FARE!

...BUT SHHHH! MUM'S THE WORD!

DON'T THINK THAT OUR PRESENCE WON'T SOON BE FELT IN THE CORRIDORS OF POWER! POLITICIANS WILL IGNORE US AT THEIR PERIL!

WHEN REAGAN AND HIS ILK DEAL WITH US, THEY'LL LEARN TO SAY 'SIR!'

SLAP SLAP...

WE HAVE WAYS OF DEALING WITH THE RECALCITRANT!...

WHAT ABOUT THE TENSIONS THAT HISTORICALLY HAVE ARISEN BETWEEN GAY MEN AND LESBIANS?

YES, IT'S TRUE THAT WE DO HAVE A FEW KINKS TO IRON OUT WITHIN OUR OWN COMMUNITY— SEXISM BEING ONE OF THEM! HOWEVER, I EXPECT A NEW ERA OF RAISED CONSCIOUSNESS TO ARRIVE WITH THE INVENTION BY CRACK SCIENTISTS IN OUR NEW GAY LABORATORIES OF...

**Panel 1:**

...SOLAR-POWERED OPPRESSION-SENSITIVE SUBJECTIVE INSIGHT-EXCHANGE HELMETS!

GEE, BETTY... NOW I UNDERSTAND YOUR POINT OF VIEW! I CAN'T BELIEVE WHAT SHALLOW, OPPRESSIVE, POWER-HUNGRY MALE-CHAUVINIST JERKS ALL OF US GUYS HAVE BEEN! WE DESERVE TO BE BANISHED TO DANTE'S MOST TERRIBLE RING OF HELL!

OH, BUT ALVIN... SUDDENLY I CAN SEE HOW I AND MY SISTERS HAVE BEEN SHRILL, UNBENDING IDEOLOGUES, UNABLE TO SYMPATHIZE WITH THE TORTURED ANGST OF MISUNDERSTOOD MALEHOOD! LET'S PUT PAST SLIGHTS BEHIND US AND WORK TOGETHER FOR THE BETTERMENT OF ALL PERSONKIND!

**Panel 2:**

THE SAME HIGH-TECH APPARATUS CAN BE USED TO FURTHER UNDERSTANDING BETWEEN DIFFERENT RACIAL, ETHNIC AND ECONOMIC GROUPS, TOO! IN FACT, IT SHOULD ULTIMATELY LET US FIND OUT EXACTLY WHAT THE SCORE IS WITH THOSE LESBIAN SEAGULLS THAT GOT ALL THAT PUBLICITY A FEW YEARS BACK...

THINK WE CAN GET THREE SECONDS OF SENSE OUTA THAT, VERNON?

HEY, LOOK, GEORGE! THAT ONE IS PERFECT!

IF WE PAD!

**Panel 3:**

ONCE AGAIN GAYS WILL BE AT THE CULTURAL FRONTIER, SPREADING PEACE AND LOVE THROUGHOUT THE WORLD, JUST AS WE DID IN THE SIXTIES WITH THE CARNABY STREET LOOK—WHA-??

WRAP HIM UP QUICK, MEN! WE MUST CAPTURE THE ESSENCE OF OUR CENTURY'S EPIC STRUGGLE BETWEEN BIGOTRY AND ENLIGHTENMENT!

GLUG!!

YOU GET HIS YIN AND I'LL GET HIS YANG!

**Panel 4:**

HEY! GET THAT THING OUTA MY NEIGHBORHOOD!

HOMAGE TO A HOMOSEXUAL VISIONARY —1984—

GEORGE SEGAL STRIKES AGAIN!

#### About the concluding panel of
### "The Gay in the Street"

Most of this exercise in prognostication from the vantage point of 1984 is self-explanatory, but its concluding flourish is likely to be puzzling to readers too young to remember the 1980s art scene.

So let me explain. The "George Segal" referenced in that panel is not the *actor* of that name (memorable in the role of Nick in the 1966 Mike Nichols film of Edward Albee's *Who's Afraid of Virginia Woolf*), but rather an identically named *sculptor* who became famous for creating statues cast from actual living-and-breathing humans willing to be swathed in plaster-soaked strips of cloth while wearing their street clothes. Although heterosexual by all accounts, Segal the sculptor (who died in 2000) created commemorative statues honoring the Gay Liberation Movement that remain on view in New York's Christopher Park at Sheridan Square, just up the street from the bar where the Stonewall riots took place.

Photo credit: Dale Hopson

HOMAGE TO A HOMOSEXUAL VISIONARY -1984-

OTHERS OF US HAVE TAKEN UP KNITTING...

STORY BEGINS ON NEXT PAGE

#### About "1986: An Interim Epilogue"

In 1986 Paul Taylor, the editor of an arts magazine in Australia called *Art & Text*, asked to reprint "Safe Sex," my 6-pager about AIDS that had run a couple of years earlier in *Gay Comix #4*. But he had an extra request: he wanted me to draw two additional pages in a similar vein reflecting the epidemic's winding path during the intervening years. "1986: An Interim Epilogue" was my response.

# 1986: an interim EPILOGUE
by Howard Cruse

IT'S NOT **ALL** BAD, FOLKS! MANY OF US HAVE SEIZED THIS **PIVOTAL** MOMENT IN **HISTORY** TO PONDER THE **SUBTLER** RAMIFICATIONS OF THE **SEXUAL** REVOLUTION AND ASSOCIATED CULTURAL PHENOMENA...

OTHERS OF US HAVE TAKEN UP **KNITTING**...

GAY HISTORY

SERIOUSLY, FOLKS, I THINK WE'VE ALL BEEN **IMPRESSED** BY THE **VIGOROUS WAY** MANY OF US HAVE RESPONDED TO THE **EPIDEMIC!**

WE'VE **MARSHALED** OUR **RESOURCES!**

WE'VE **CHANGED** OUR **BEHAVIOR** WHERE CHANGE WAS **CALLED** FOR!

**REALLY!!** WE'VE BEEN **SUPER!!**

©1986 by H. Cruse.

BUT THERE'S BEEN NO **LET-UP** IN THE **CRAZINESS** SINCE '83! NO SIRREE!

PLENTY OF **GRIST** FOR MY ACERBIC **MILL!**

...LIKE TH' **FEDS' TIGHT WALLET** IN TH' **A.I.D.S. RESEARCH** DEPARTMENT! DO **THEY** CARE THAT WE'RE **DYIN'?** NOT **RONNIE** & COMPANY!

THEN THERE WAS TH' **ROCK HUDSON** EPISODE!

Scribble sketch!...

COULD IT BE ALL THOSE **GERBILS** WE'VE BEEN PUTTING UP OUR **ASSES?**

GEE... I NEVE THOUGH OF THA

AND TH' **AFRICAN SWINE FEVER** WARS!

HARD TO KNOW WHAT **ANGLE** TO TAKE...

THE SEARCH FOR A CO-FACTOR

FOUR YEARS INTO THE HEALTH CRISIS, THE PRESIDENT OF THE UNITED STATES ACTUALLY UTTERS THE WORD 'A.I.D.S.' IN PUBLIC... ONCE!

I CAN'T OVERLOOK **HTLV-III ANTIBODY TESTING**...WHICH BRINGS UP TH' **CONFIDENTIALITY** ISSUE... JEEZ, THAT'S THREE OR FOUR **PANELS** I'VE USED UP RIGHT **THERE!**

DID I DREAM THAT, KIP..?

THE MORAL ORITY HOLDS PRAYER REAKFAST... LL TOGETHER OW: **GOD**, WE THANK THEE THAT WE ARE NOT AS **OTHER** MEN ARE...

AND WHAT ABOUT **VIRUS PIRACY** AMONG THE **LAB SMOCK** SET?

AND I THINK ONCE EVERY TEN OR TWENTY THOUSAND DEATHS IS QUITE **ENOUGH**, THANK YOU!

IT'S FUNNY THE WAY I KEEP STEPPING INTO CHILLY **AIR** POCKETS...

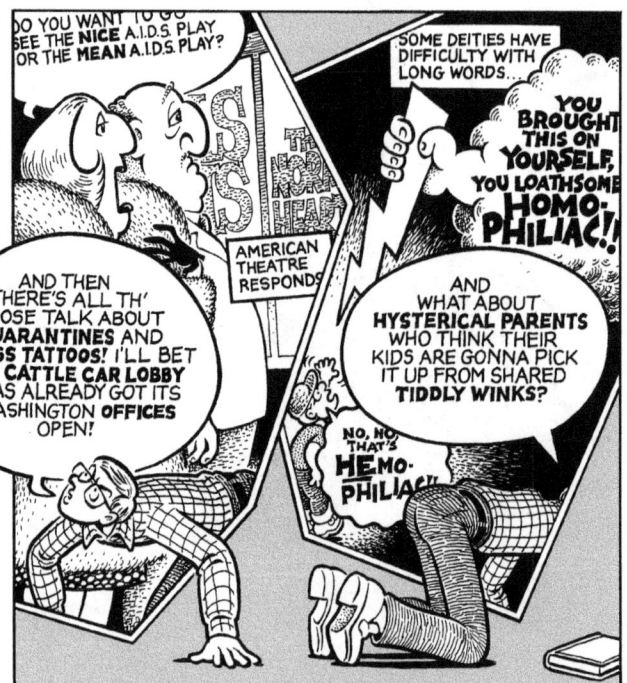

GERA CUST ON T

DO YOU WANT TO GO SEE THE **NICE** A.I.D.S. PLAY OR THE **MEAN** A.I.D.S. PLAY?

SOME DEITIES HAVE DIFFICULTY WITH LONG WORDS...

AMERICAN THEATRE RESPONDS

**YOU BROUGHT THIS ON YOURSELF**, YOU LOATHSOME **HOMO-PHILIAC!!**

AND THEN THERE'S ALL TH' LOOSE TALK ABOUT **QUARANTINES** AND **MASS TATTOOS!** I'LL BET TH' **CATTLE CAR LOBBY** HAS ALREADY GOT ITS WASHINGTON **OFFICES** OPEN!

AND WHAT ABOUT **HYSTERICAL PARENTS** WHO THINK THEIR KIDS ARE GONNA PICK IT UP FROM SHARED **TIDDLY WINKS?**

NO, NO, THAT'S **HE**MO-PHILIAC!!

## George,

*Who played with a Dangerous Toy, and suffered a Catastrophe of considerable Dimensions.*

When George's Grandmamma was told

## Lord Lundy,

*Who was too Freely Moved to Tears, and thereby ruined his Political Career.*

## Henry King,

*Who chewed bits of String, and was early cut off in Dreadful Agonies.*

The Chief Defect of Henry King
Was chewing little bits of String.
At last he swallowed some which tied
Itself in ugly Knots inside.

...om his earliest years
...eely moved to Tears.
..." his Mother said,
...time to go to Bed!"

# BACKSTORY

### About "Penceworth"

*A local authority "shall not intentionally promote homosexuality or publish material with the intention of promoting homosexuality" or "promote the teaching in any maintained school of the acceptability of homosexuality as a pretended family relationship."*

—Anti-gay legislation, widely known as "Clause 28," that was passed by Great Britain's Parliament in 1988.

*AARGH** was a benefit comic book that was published in the U.K. to raise funds for combatting Clause 28. I and cartoonists from several nations drew contributions.

My text for "Penceworth" mimics the versifying style used by Hilaire Belloc (1870-1953) in his classic *Cautionary Verses*, which were themselves deadpan spoofs of existing morality tales for children. My drawings for the story channeled as best I could manage a hybrid of the styles of two illustrators who provided drawings for Belloc's book: Nicholas Bentley and the enigmatically credited "B.T.B."

*\*Artists Against Rampant Government Homophobia*

WITHOUT WARNING, THE SPIRITUAL ENTITY ONCE KNOWN AS **HILAIRE BELLOC** (1870-1953) — or an impertinent impersonator thereof — IS CHANNELED THROUGH THE CARTOONIST KNOWN AS **HOWARD CRUSE**, RESULTING IN THE NEWLY MINTED **CAUTIONARY VERSE** WHICH FOLLOWS...

©1988 by H. Cruse

# Penceworth,

*Who, inspired by the Widely Reviled*
*Antisocial Behavior of a certain German Dictator whose*
*Name need not be mentioned here, Behaved*
*Unkindly to his Fellow Man on no basis more substantive*
*than the Offender's Sexual Orientation, and in Rueful Consequence*
*loosed upon himself the Entirely Appropriate Opprobrium*
*of all the Civilized World,*
*his Grandmother included.*

by Howard Cruse

When little Penceworth was a tyke,
He found a tome on Hitler's *Reich*
Which documented every trait
Of that most horrid Chief-of-State.

Enamoured of the *Führer*'s knack
For Oratorical Attack,
He goose-stepped to the Parlor where
He chirped *"Sieg heil!"* to his *grand-mère*.

Published in *AARGH*

To his chagrin, she was displeased
By play so Loathsome and Diseased
And, grabbing for the nearest broom,
She smacked Penceworth across the room.

"How dare you don the dreadful shoes
Of one who so abused the Jews?"

The chastened Penceworth wept and swore
To honour Jews forevermore.

And to his word was Penceworth true:
He tipped his hat to every Jew.

Redeeming thus his youth misspent,
He soon was sent to Parliament.

But Wicked Seeds in childhood sown
Arise to flower when we're grown.
While gracing Jews
with lavish praise,

Penceworth behaved less well to Gays.

Towards all
whom Penceworth deemed perverse
He vented Crude Remarks and worse,
Inflicting on them Evil Tricks,
And sometimes pumm'ling them with Bricks.

Whene'er a Bachelor crossed his path,
He thought the worst and quaked with Wrath;

And Spinsters, loath to marry young,
Were met with Scorn and duly hung.

No matter that they spoke with wit
Or strove to make his Waistcoat fit;
No matter that they served him tea
Or won awards at Forestry;

No matter that they fed the Poor
Or healed the Soldiers, back from war,

Or elegantly mimicked Rage
With Graceful Swordplay on the stage;

No matter that they worshipped Art,
Reciting Belloc's Verse by heart;
Or washed and waxed the Royal Coach —

He could but view them with reproach
And call for misbegotten Laws
To mounting waves of shrill applause
From Journalists of Ill Repute

(Who loved the chance to Persecute).

Alas, good fortune cannot smile
For long upon a wretch so Vile.
One morning, rising from his rest,
He found his face with Moustache blest.

And not a Handsome one by far,
No grandly arching handlebar,
But one so Ugly and so Square
It looked like Hitler's very Hair.

"Oh, woe!" he wept, "what Monster grows
Unwelcomed underneath my nose?"
And set about to scrape and clip
The Fibrous Fungus from his lip.

But though he clipped
    and though he plucked,
The *Führer*'s Face
    would not be shucked.
And thenceforth all who saw his face
Could not but retch at his Disgrace.

And that included his *grand-mère*,
Who, on her deathbed, saw him there
And, drawing on her final Breath,
Beat Penceworth, with her broom,
                    to death.

THE MORAL

Impressionable lads of Eight
Should Take Care whom they Emulate.

CRUSE

78

## About **"The Kardinal & The Klansman"**

Relations between New York's LGBT community and John Cardinal O'Connor were endlessly adversarial. O'Connor was appointed by a Pope who wanted hard-headed orthodoxy at St. Patrick's Cathedral and O'Connor took that mission seriously. "The Kardinal & The Klansman" was occasioned by word that O'Connor was industrously organizing phone banks to combat passage in 1986 of a gay rights bill that had been engaging activists for fifteen years. The good news is that phone calls failed to thwart historical momentum and the bill became law that year.

Published in *The Village Voice*

About **"Homoeroticism Blues"**

> *"None of the funds authorized to be appropriated [by the NEA] may be used to promote, disseminate, or produce materials which in the judgment of the National Endowment for the Arts....may be considered obscene, including but not limited to depictions of sadomasochism,* homoeroticism, *the sexual exploitation of children, or individuals engaged in sex acts..."*
>
> —Language added to the 1989 Senate Appropriations Bill at the behest of the famously homophobic U.S. Senator Jesse Helms, reacting in part to proposed but hastily aborted NEA funding for an exhibit of Robert Mapplethorpe's sexually transgressive photographs (with emphasis added by me).

Published in *Artforum International*

 **BACKSTORY**

About
**"The Woeful World of Winnie & Walt"**
(begins on following page)

This strip references a complacency-inducing article by Dr. Robert E. Gould in the January 1988 issue of *Cosmopolitan* entitled "Reassuring News About AIDS: A Doctor Tells Why You May Not Be At Risk." The article was characterized as "clearly not based on the known facts" as well as "potentially dangerous" by Dr. Anthony Fauci of the National Institutes of Health.

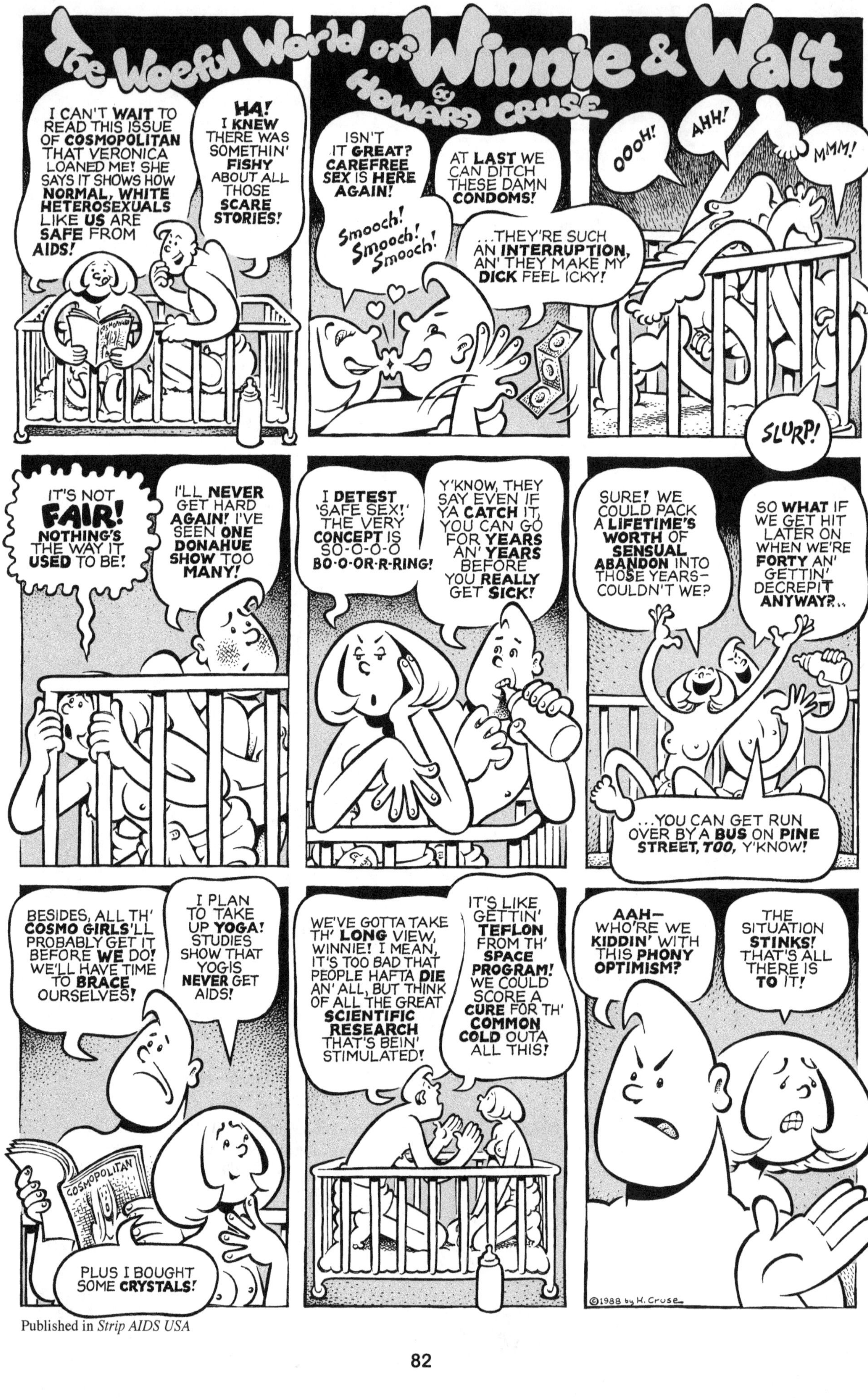


Published in *Strip AIDS USA*

Published in *The Village Voice*

# Rainbow Curriculum Comix

≥ Snicker! ≤ HERE COMES THAT BIG YELLOW BIRD!

HIS VOICE IS ALL GIRLY-GIRLY!

NOBODY'S EVER SEEN HIM GO OUT ON A DATE!

ALL HIS FRIENDS HAVE DIED OF AIDS, I HEAR!

...NOW HE WANTS TO TURN EVERYBODY ELSE INTO SISSYBIRDS SO THEY CAN DIE TOO!

GET OUTA TOWN, BEAK-SUCKER!

DON'T LET HIM MOLT ON YOU!

N-NO! PLEASE DON'T HIT ME! Pow! Stab! Eeeek!

♪ SUNN·N·NY DAY...KEEPIN' THE QUEERS AWAY... ♪

©1993 by Howard Cruse

TODAY'S EDITION OF 'SODOMY STREET' HAS BEEN MADE POSSIBLE BY THE DISTRICT 24 SCHOOL BOARD OF THE NEW YORK CITY SCHOOL SYSTEM... AND BY VIEWERS LIKE YOU!!

WHAT'S ON NEXT?

'REV. ROBERTSON'S NEIGHBOR-HOOD.'

Published in the *Gay Community News*
Special 1993 March on Washington edition

## BACKSTORY

### About **"Rainbow Curriculum Comix"** (at left) and **"The Educator"** (following page)

In 1992 Mary Cummins, President of School District 24 in New York City's borough of Queens, generated a firestorm of bigotry when Joseph Fernandez, the city's Schools Chancellor, introduced a diversity-affirming curriculum called the *Children of the Rainbow*, which included matter-of-fact recognition at all grade levels of the existence of gay people in the community and an acknowledgment that among the class-mates of any student may be some who have gay or lesbian parents.

As a result of Ms. Cummins's inflammatory oratory and strident mass-mailings to District 24 parents (paid for with school funds), passions ruled the day and the proposed curriculum was discarded.

Once the dust had settled Fernandez resigned and departed the city for saner pastures.

**COMMUNITY SCHOOL BOARD 24**
67-54 80th Street
Middle Village, New York 11379

*Memorandum*

Date August 28, 1992

To: Parents, Community School District 24

Subject:

This is a follow-up to last month's alert about the protest outside 110 Livingston Street that District 24 plans against the curriculum mandated by Chancellor Fernandez called "Children of the Rainbow, First Grade". This curriculum would have teachers telling their first-graders that gay/lesbian couples are "family" just like any other family unit. We will not accept two people of the same sex engaged in deviant sex practices as "family". Some of the books recommended to be read to or by the children are "Heather Has Two Mommies", "Daddy's Roommate", "Gloria Goes to Gay Pride".

Now to another curriculum [...] called "educator", Joseph Fernandez. It is [...] of the HIV virus and AIDS to be [...] st [...] ims of this AIDS se [...] rs of illicit [...] to their [...] the Chancellor [...] ns and refers to [...] rate of failure [...] teaching our [...] the only sure [...] kids that sodomy

[...] OCTOBER 6. BUSES [...] YOU WILL JOIN US. [...] SCHOOL BOARD 24, [...] ADVISE THAT THEY [...] WITH THE TIME AND [...] AREAS BETWEEN

*Mary*

Mary A. Cummins
President

### Queens School Board Prez Calls Gays 'Deviant'

Calling gays "deviant," Queens District 24 School Board president Mary Cummins fired the most recent shot in a stand-off between the conservative school district and gay activists. The two sides have been at war over the citywide "Children of the Rainbow" multicultural curriculum, which the Queens district has refused to adopt on the basis of its references to lesbian and gay parented families.

In an Aug. 28 letter to district p[...] Cummins writes, "we will not accept two [...] the same sex engaged in deviant sex [...] 'family." Cummins also blasts School [...] Joseph Fernandez, who supports th[...] Fernandez, she wrote, "would tea[...] sodomy is acceptable but that w[...] thing weird."

Fernandez's spokesman, F[...] the statement "ludicrous" an[...] curacies." He pointed out th[...] charges erroneously con[...] the Rainbow" curriculum [...]

### New York Newsday

#### EDITORIALS

### New Sideshow
#### How to waste school funds

Cummins

Never mind the kindergarten classes with 50 kids. Or the classes held in bathrooms and stairwells because of overcrowding. Never mind the thousands of immigrant children struggling to learn a new language. Or the acute shortage of books and chairs. Why grapple with those fundamental problems in western Queens when you can [...] source school dollars to mak [...] one: "He [chancellor] [...] would teach [...]

# The EDUCATOR

**Panel 1:** WHY ARE THOSE PEOPLE MAKING SUCH A **FUSS** DOWN THERE IN THE **STREET**, MISS PEONY?

**Panel 2:** WHY ARE THEY SMEARING **BOILING TAR** AND **FEATHERS** ON THAT **MAN** DOWN THERE?

COME AWAY FROM THE **WINDOW**, JOHNNY, AND I'LL **EXPLAIN EVERYTHING.**

**Panel 3:** **TARRING-AND-FEATHERING** PEOPLE AND THEN RUNNING THEM **LICKETY-SPLIT** OUT OF TOWN ON A **RAIL** IS THE WAY WE LET THEM KNOW NOT TO SAY THINGS **OUT LOUD** THAT **CHILDREN** SHOULDN'T **HEAR.**

BYE-BYE, MISTER....

**Panel 4:** THE MAN IS BEING **PUNISHED** FOR NOT KEEPING A **SECRET**, YOU SEE.

A **SECRET**?

YES, DEAR.

**Panel 5:** THERE ARE A SET OF **PEOPLE** IN THE WORLD WHO ARE SO **AWFUL** THAT WE'RE ALL SUPPOSED TO KEEP IT A **SECRET** THAT THEY **EXIST.**

Y'MEAN THOSE PEOPLE WHO ARE WAVING THEIR **FISTS** AND **SNARLING** AT THE MAN ON THE RAIL?

NO, **THOSE** ARE THE **GOOD** PEOPLE YOU SHOULD GROW UP AND BE **LIKE.**

**Panel 6:** THEN WHO ARE THE "**AWFUL** PEOPLE"?

*NO, NO, NO*

YOU MUSTN'T ASK ME TO TELL SECRETS WHILE WE'RE IN **SCHOOL.**

**Panel 7:** IF YOU WANT TO KNOW WHO I'M **TALKING** ABOUT YOU'LL HAVE TO LISTEN TO ME ON THE **SIX O'CLOCK NEWS**, READ THE **LETTERS** I SEND TO YOUR **MOMMY** AND **DADDY**, WATCH ME DELIVER **SPEECHES** AT **HATE RALLIES**, OR LISTEN TO YOUR FRIENDS CALL EACH OTHER '**FAGGOT**' DURING **RECESS!**

**Panel 8:** THE MAN ON THE RAIL IS BEING ASKED TO LEAVE FOR BEING **IRRESPONSIBLE** AND TRYING TO **LIE** AND SAY THESE PEOPLE **EXIST** WHEN THE **REST** OF US HAVE AGREED TO SAY THEY **DON'T.**

YOU HAVE TO **KNOW** THAT THEY DON'T **EXIST** SO YOU WON'T GROW UP TO BE **LIKE** THEM.

**Panel 9:** YOU NEED TO STAY **AWAY** FROM THESE PEOPLE THAT DON'T EXIST BECAUSE OF THEIR TERRIBLE **DISEASES** THAT ARE MAKING THEM **DIE.**

THEY WANT TO **RECRUIT YOU** TO BE **LIKE** THEM SO THAT **YOU** CAN DIE, **TOO.**

**THAT'S** NOT NICE, IS IT?

NO, MA'AM.

**Panel 10:** AND IT'S **DANGEROUS** TO BE **AROUND** THEM EVEN IF YOU **DON'T** LET THEM RECRUIT YOU. THEY SQUIRT THEIR **TAINTED BLOOD** AND **POISONOUS BODY FLUIDS** THIS WAY AND THAT LIKE A **LAWN SPRINKLER.**

**Panel 11:** THE MAN ON THE RAIL WANTED TO TELL YOU THAT YOU COULD MAKE YOURSELF **SAFER** WITH LITTLE PIECES OF RUBBER CALLED '**CONDOMS**'...

...BUT IT'S **IMPORTANT** THAT YOU **NOT** KNOW THAT **CONDOMS** EXIST **EITHER**...

**Panel 12:** ...BECAUSE **THEN** YOU MIGHT LEARN THAT YOU HAVE A **PENIS**, AND **THAT** WOULD MAKE GOD **SAD.**

OH, MY...I'VE **UPSET** YOU, HAVEN'T I?

**Panel 13:** DON'T **WORRY.** THE MEAN MAN ON THE RAIL IS **GONE** NOW.

*Smack!*

*Sniff!*

**Panel 14:** YOU WON'T NEED TO KNOW ABOUT THE **AWFUL** PEOPLE WHO DON'T EXIST UNTIL YOU'RE A **TEENAGER** AND CAN CHASE THEM DOWN WITH **BASEBALL BATS.**

**Panel 15:** NOW OPEN UP YOUR **READER**, DEAR. DICK AND JANE ARE **WAITING** FOR YOU.

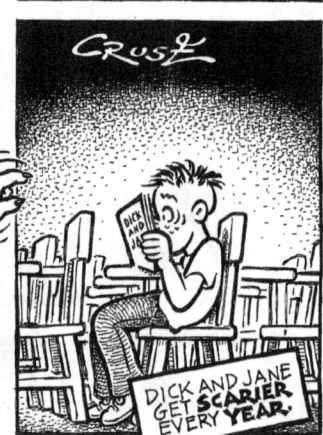

©2009 H. Cruse

**Panel 16:** CRUSE

DICK AND JANE GET **SCARIER** EVERY **YEAR.**

Scripted and sketched in 1993 and completed for inclusion in this book

# Where are Wendel & Toland?
## 1983-96

**W**endel Trupstock and Toland Polk are as gay as any other characters in this collection, but none of their exploits are on hand here since they have their own books (*The Complete Wendel* and *Stuck Rubber Baby*) to hang out in.

# Late Entries
## 2000-08

**A** lot of mundane practical obstacles, not to mention big and ongoing changes in the marketplace for comics and cartoons, have left me short on opportunities to draw comics since *Stuck Rubber Baby* was published—on *any* topics, much less gay ones!

**D**espite the aforementioned impediments, however, I do have three more gay-themed strips to offer in the pages that follow. Naturally I expect to draw more such comics in the future, which is why I have refrained from characterizing this book as a "complete" collection of my gay work. Why clamp a period onto the end of a sentence when there's clearly a lot yet to be said?

**S**till, books have to have endings and I'm closing this book with my memory of a sexy guy I'm calling "Claude," who may or may not be a minister at that church just down the block from you.

**B**ut first let's spend time (*a*) at a zoo and (*b*) under the spell of a hypnotist.

## BACKSTORY

### About "A Zoo of Our Own"

Gay sex among the animal set? Sure, we all heard about those lesbian seagulls a while back, but who can tell what sex any given bird is anyway, what with all those feathers obscuring its pubes?

Well, since gull-on-gull mating first made headlines, additional loose talk about homosexual coupling (and family building) in the animal kingdom has persisted. Such talk gained added credence in 1999 with the publication of Dr. Bruce Bagemihl's *Biological Exuberance*: *Animal Homosexuality and Natural Diversity*.

I was skeptical when the *Village Voice* commissioned me to illustrate my personal take on gay animals with a full-page, full-color comic strip to run in the tabloid's 2001 Gay Pride issue. But I dutifully read the Bagemihl book in preparation for this assignment and found its argument more persuasive than I had expected. Also, its literal zoological premise made an appealing jumping-off place for some riffs on gay ways among humans.

"A Zoo of Our Own" was approved but then, alas, got bumped from the *Voice* at the last minute. So although it's been viewable on my web site for a while, this is its first print publication.

I have reconfigured the strip, by the way, from its original single-page format (see above) to the four-page version that follows. This was necessary to keep its lettering readable, since reducing the tabloid-sized version enough to fit entirely on one of these smaller pages would almost certainly have led to eyestrain.

### About "My Hypnotist" (pp. 93-97) and "Then There Was Claude" (p. 98)

The final two stories in this book were originally published in full color, an indulgence that isn't practical in this collection. Their color versions can be found respectively in *Young Bottoms in Love* (edited by Tim Fish, 2007, Poison Press) and *Born to Trouble: Book of Boy Trouble 2* (edited by Robert Kirby and David Kelly, 2008, Green Candy Press).

# A ZOO of our OWN

When hip editors get wind of a story, they know who to CALL!

HEY, CRUSE, THE WEB IS BUZZING ABOUT A NEW ZOO FOR GAY ANIMALS THEY'VE SET UP IN AMSTERDAM!

I'M ON IT, CHIEF!

Chuckle! WHERE DO THESE SILLY INTERNET HOAXES COME FROM?

Howard Cruse Investigative Cartoonist

BUT IS IT A HOAX?

WHAT IF IT'S (gasp) TRUE??

STRANGER THINGS HAVE HAPPENED!

OBVIOUSLY, THIS CALLS FOR A MEASURED SOCIO-BIOLOGICAL ANALYSIS...

...STARTING WITH RIGOROUS RESEARCH FROM THE FIELD.

SAY, FOXY... SPEAKING AS A REPRESENTATIVE OF THE ANIMAL KINGDOM, WHAT'S YOUR POSITION ON GAY ZOOS?

FOXY'S RIGHT. HOW COULD A 'PET' SPEAK FREELY ABOUT SEXUAL ORIENTATION ISSUES WITH HER 'OWNER'? THE POWER DIFFERENTIAL IS TOO GREAT.

I SHOULD TALK TO SOME ANIMALS IN THE NEIGHBORHOOD THAT I DON'T KNOW PERSON-ALLY.

OH, SURE! LIKE I'M ABOUT TO SPEAK MY MIND AND RUN AFOUL OF SOME TRENDY POLITICAL AGENDA OF YOURS? I THINK NOT!

HAPPILY, HERE IN NEW YORK, DIVERSE POINTS OF VIEW ARE ALWAYS NEAR AT HAND.

Unpublished except as a feature at www.howardcruse.com

Biological Exuberance by Bruce Bagemihl, Ph.D.
St. Martin's Press, 2000

91

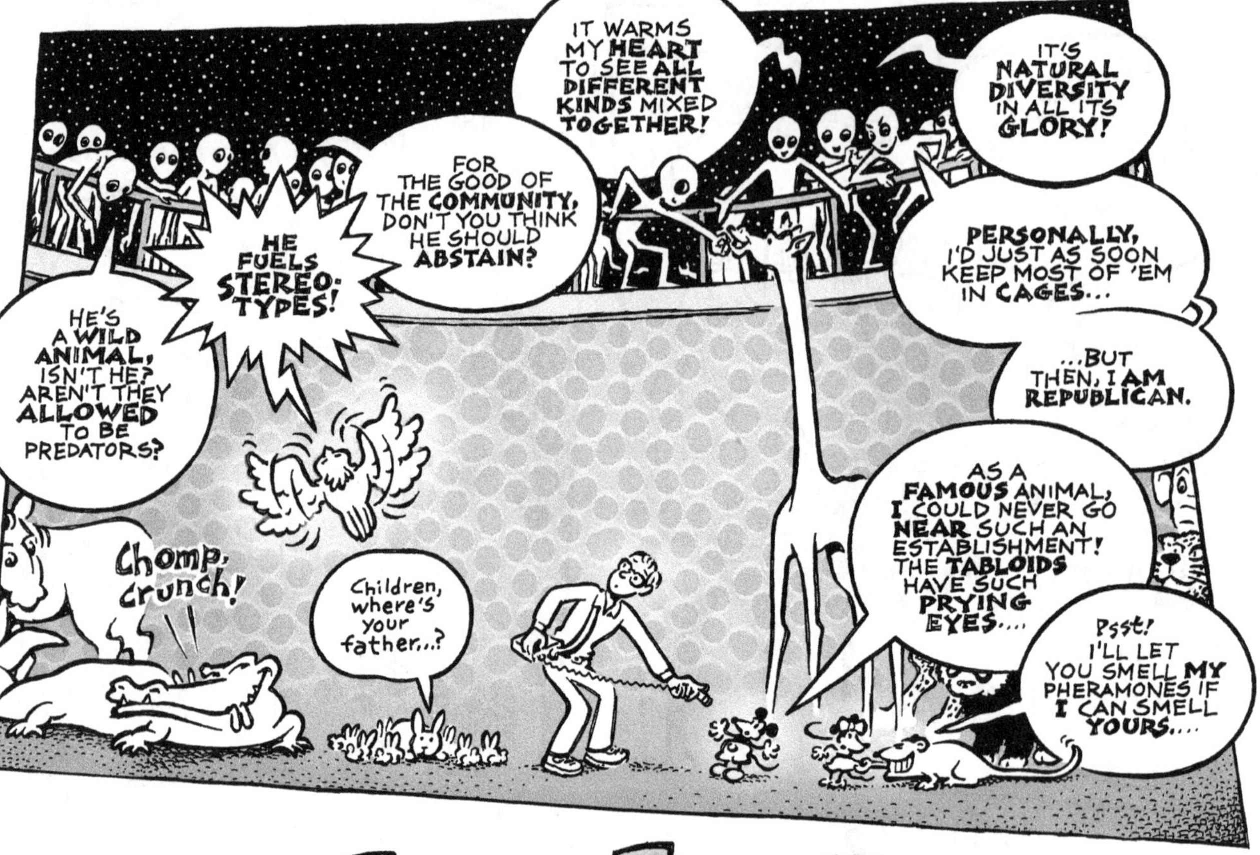


# *FOXY'S FOOTNOTE

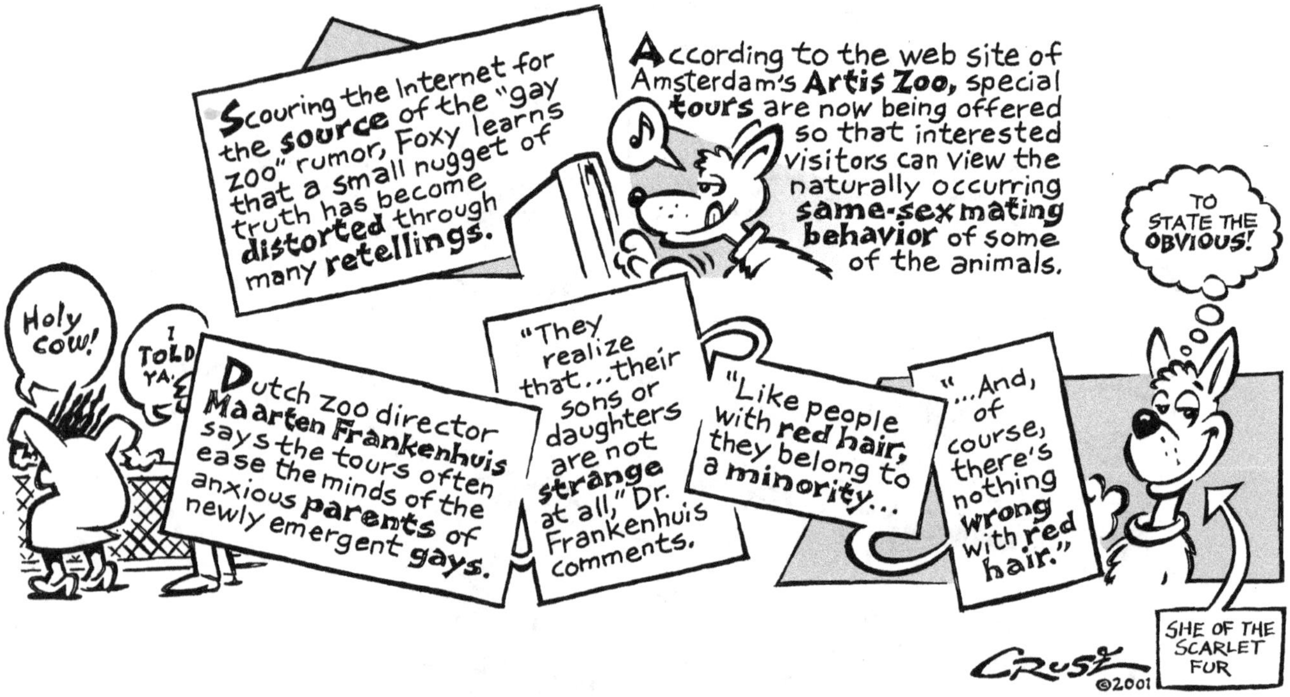

## *Foxy's Footnote

Scouring the Internet for the **source** of the "gay zoo" rumor, Foxy learns that a small nugget of truth has become **distorted** through many **retellings**.

According to the web site of Amsterdam's **Artis Zoo**, special **tours** are now being offered so that interested visitors can view the naturally occurring **same-sex mating behavior** of some of the animals.

TO STATE THE **OBVIOUS!**

Holy cow!

I TOLD YA!

**D**utch zoo director **Maarten Frankenhuis** says the tours often ease the minds of the anxious **parents** of newly emergent **gays**.

"They realize that....their sons or daughters are not **strange** at all," Dr. Frankenhuis comments.

"Like people with **red hair**, they belong to a **minority**...

"...And, of course, there's nothing **wrong** with red hair."

SHE OF THE SCARLET FUR

Crus ©2001

MY HYPNOTISM

by Howard Cruse ©2005

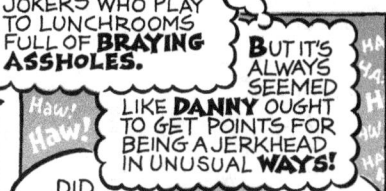

Published in *Young Bottoms in Love*

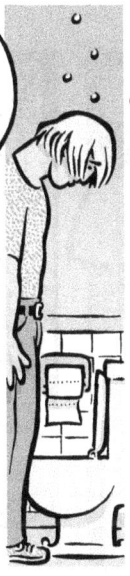

Then There Was Claude

GLAUDE WAS THE FIRST GUY I WENT TO **BED** WITH WHO I BEGAN TO THINK MIGHT HAVE **LONG-TERM BOYFRIEND** POTENTIAL.

I WAS SO **TURNED ON** BY HIM, IT **HURT!**

THEN CLAUDE MENTIONED THAT HE WAS STUDYING FOR THE **MINISTRY** AT A LOCAL **BIBLE COLLEGE.**

YER GONNA BE A **PREACHER?!**

YEAH.

BUT DOESN'T TH' CHURCH SAY THAT YOU AND I ARE GONNA GO TO **HELL** FOR BEIN' **GAY?**

TECHNICALLY.

ISN'T THAT A **PROBLEM** FOR YOU?

NAH.

I'LL BE 100% **STRAIGHT** ON **SUNDAYS.** WHAT MY CONGREGATION DOESN'T KNOW ABOUT THE **REST** OF MY WEEK WON'T **HURT** IT.

AFTER THAT I BEGAN HAVING SOME **DOUBTS** THAT CLAUDE WAS GONNA MAKE GOOD **BOY-FRIEND** MATERIAL...

...AND I WASN'T ALL **THAT** SURE HE WAS GONNA MAKE GOOD **MINISTER** MATERIAL, EITHER.

Mmmm... BABY, THOSE **EYES** OF YOURS ARE SO **BLUE,** THEY DRIVE ME **CRAAAZEEE...**

Crusz ©2008

THE **SEX** WAS GOOD, THOUGH, WHILE IT LASTED.

Published in *Born To Trouble* / *Book of Boy Trouble Volume 2*

## About Howard Cruse

**HOWARD CRUSE**'s comic strips and humorous illustrations have appeared in numerous books and national magazines since he launched his career in underground comic books in the 1970s.

Cruse was the founding editor in 1980 of the underground comix series *Gay Comix*. He is most widely known for the *Advocate*'s 1980s comic strip series *Wendel* and the international award-winning graphic novel *Stuck Rubber Baby*.

Cruse and his husband, Ed Sedarbaum, presently reside with Lulu the dalmatian in northwestern Massachusetts.

*www.howardcruse.com*

## About *Felix's Friends*
### A STORY FOR GROWN-UPS AND UNPLEASANT CHILDREN

Cruse's newly repackaged 1986 tale about a buoyantly bothersome brat is available exclusively from the Lulu Marketplace online.

*www.lulu.com/content/2603474*

### *Mugs! Tee-shirts!*
### *Mousepads & More!*

*www.cafepress.com/crusegoodies*